GREAT AMERICAN STORIES 2

Third Edition

C.G. Draper

Great American Stories 2: An ESL/EFL Reader

Third Edition

Pearson Education, 10 Bank Street, White Plains, NY 10606

Vice president, director of publishing: Allen Ascher
Editorial director: Louisa Hellegers
Acquisitions editor: Laura Le Dréan
Senior development manager: Penny Laporte
Development editor: Paula H. Van Ells
Vice president, director of design and production: Rhea Banker
Executive managing editor: Linda Moser
Associate production editor: Melissa Leyva
Production supervisor: Ray Keating
Senior manufacturing buyer: Dave Dickey
Cover design: Elizabeth Carlson
Cover image: Images.com/Spots on the Spot/Herzberg, Tom
Text design: Jill Yutkowitz
Text composition: Rainbow Graphics
Text art: Charles Shaw

Library of Congress Cataloging-in-Publication Data

Draper, C.G.
    Great American stories 2 / C.G. Draper.—3rd ed.
      p. cm.
    Intermediate adapted short stories with exercises.
    ISBN 0-13-030960-5 (alk. paper)
    1. English language—Textbooks for foreign speakers. 2. Short stories,
American—Adaptations. 3. Readers—United States. I. Title: Great American
stories two.
PE1128 .D675 2001b
428.6'4—dc21

2001022744

7 8 9 10–CW–09 08 07

CONTENTS

TO THE TEACHER

GREAT AMERICAN STORIES 2 consists of eight careful adaptations of famous stories by classic American writers with exercises for each story in reading skills, vocabulary, word forms, language activities, writing, and discussion. Prereading exercises introduce the student to the world of the story and help develop the student's reading skills in scanning and skimming. One of the prereading exercises in each chapter is based on the biographical information about the story's author on the title page of each story.

A Key Words paragraph gives a brief introduction to the story using several words that are central to readers' understanding of the story. Each key word (in **boldface** in the paragraph) is at least partially defined by the context in the paragraph. Since the skill of guessing a word's basic meaning from context is an important one for the intermediate student to develop, the teacher would do well to review this paragraph with the students before beginning the story.

The stories in the book are both graded and progressive—that is, the vocabulary, grammar, and internal structure of the stories increase in difficulty from the first story (which is at the intermediate level of proficiency) to the last (which is at the high-intermediate level). Structural, lexical, and sentence-length controls have been used throughout the book. The head-word list for the first two stories contains 1,000 words; for the next four stories, 1,500 words; and for the final two stories, 2,000 words. Maximum sentence length increases from fifteen words in the first story to twenty-five in the last, and new grammatical structures are added story by story. Words from outside the head-word lists are introduced in a context that helps make their meaning clear; they are used again within the next 100 words of text and then repeated at least two more times before the end of the story.

The book as a whole is designed to be incorporated into a twelve- to fourteen-week ESL or EFL course as part of the reading program. The material can be used in or out of class—as a core reading text, ancillary text, or pleasure reading. In class, it can be used interactively, with the teacher leading the discussion or with the students working together.

Like the stories, the exercises in the book increase in difficulty, gradually introducing the student to the more demanding elements of English prose that characterize unabridged or advanced texts: irony, implication and inference, hidden meaning, figurative language, and the like. Further, the exercises are designed so that the student must constantly return to the text to check comprehension or vocabulary. An objective of the book is to involve the reader deeply in each story and the words of its writer and, toward that end, to present exercises that are difficult if not impossible to complete without a thorough understanding of the text.

Each story is divided into two or three parts. The first exercise following each story, Understanding the Plot, encompasses the entire story. It is followed by two or more Close Reading exercises that draw the student's attention to details in the separate parts of the story or to features of the language used. It is best, therefore, to have the student read through the entire story once, share first impressions, and attempt the first exercise. The student should then reread each part carefully and work on the Close Reading exercises based on the material in that section. The first long reading "stretches" the student; the rereading and exercises consolidate gains and help the student achieve complete familiarity with the material. If the student has trouble with Understanding the Plot the first time around, he or she should be asked to repeat it after the other exercises but before the Discussion exercise.

C.G.D.

TO THE READER

This book starts at the intermediate level and ends at the high-intermediate level. The eight stories in the book steadily increase in difficulty. The vocabulary list for the first two stories contains 1,000 words; for the next four stories, 1,500 words; and for the final two stories, 2,000 words. Moreover, the length of the sentences increases, and new grammar is introduced with each story.

By working on this book, you will improve your reading, speaking and discussion, vocabulary, knowledge of word forms, and writing.

Each chapter begins with a paragraph about the author of the story. You will be asked some questions that help you think about the general subject of the story. And you will do an exercise that helps you develop special reading skills. Finally, you will read a paragraph that introduces the story and some Key Words that you should know in order to understand the story.

Each story in the book is divided into two or three parts. Following the story, there is an exercise, Understanding the Plot, that is based on the whole story. This exercise is followed by Close Reading exercises on two or more sections of the story. These Close Reading exercises draw your attention to important details in the story and to important uses of the English language. You should try to read the whole story before beginning any of the exercises. If you find Understanding the Plot difficult, reread the story by sections and do the Close Reading exercises for each separate section. Then try again to do Understanding the Plot.

The remaining exercises that follow each story will help you develop your language skills in general and your reading skills in particular. The exercises are on reading comprehension, vocabulary, word forms, language use, discussion, and writing.

The stories in this book were written many years ago by eight of America's most famous writers. In reading their stories and information about their lives, you will learn interesting things about American history, daily life, and culture.

C.G.D.

THE ROMANCE OF A BUSY BROKER

✴

Adapted from the story by
O. HENRY

O. Henry was born in Greensboro, North Carolina, in 1862. His real name was William Sydney Porter. He left school at the age of fifteen and worked at different times in a drugstore, a business office, a building designer's office, and finally a bank. When he was caught taking money from his own bank, he was arrested and put in prison for three years. He had begun writing, and while he was in prison he published a book of adventure stories called *Cabbages and Kings*. He moved to New York in 1902, and it was there that he became famous for his short stories with surprise endings. He wrote hundreds of stories about the ordinary people of New York City. His most famous books include *The Four Million* and *The Voice of the City*. O. Henry died in 1910.

caught = p.p of catch

adventure : ۱. سرگذشت؛ خاطره؛ ماجراجویی ۲. ریسک، خطر کردن
خود را به خطر انداختن ۳.

adventurer : اهل ماجرا، ماجراجو

BEFORE YOU READ THE STORY

A. About the Author

Read the paragraph about O. Henry on page 1. What do you notice about his work experience? What would you expect the characters in his stories to be like?

B. The Picture

Several of the key words introduced on page 3 are shown in the picture on page 5. The **stockbroker** is reading stock prices from the **ticker tape** that was produced by the small machine on his desk. This **ticker tape machine** was in use a hundred years ago. What sort of machine would you expect to find in a stockbroker's office today? What else in the picture shows us that the story is a hundred years old?

C. Thinking About the World of Business

What do you like, or dislike, about the world of business? Why? Which of the following words or phrases best describe the business world to you: *peaceful, exciting, pressure-filled, beautiful, interesting, dangerous, busy, slow, loving, restful, fast.* Are you a businessman or a businesswoman? Would you like to be one? Why or why not?

D. Scanning for Information

Reading quickly to find small pieces of information is called *scanning.* Read the questions below. The answer to each question can be found in the paragraph about O. Henry on page 1. As you read the paragraph, look for the piece of information that will answer the question. You do not need to understand everything in the paragraph. But you must read carefully enough to find the answer to each question. Try to answer each question in thirty seconds or less.

1. In what state was O. Henry born?
2. Who was William Sydney Porter?
3. In what year did he leave school?
4. Where did he work before he began writing?
5. Where was O. Henry when he published his first book?
6. What kind of book was it?
7. What kind of stories is O. Henry most famous for?
8. What kinds of people usually appear in his stories?

A **romance** is a type of story that contains unusual or surprising events and is often about love. This romance by O. Henry is about a **broker**, or **stockbroker**—a person who buys and sells parts of businesses called **stocks** or **shares**. Years ago, brokers followed the daily buying and selling of stocks with the help of a **ticker tape machine**. This machine received the changing prices of stocks and then printed them out on thin paper (ticker tape).

THE ROMANCE OF A BUSY BROKER

I

Pitcher had worked for many years in the office of Harvey Maxwell, the stockbroker. Pitcher was a quiet man. He didn't usually let his face show his feelings. But this morning he looked surprised—and very interested. Harvey Maxwell had arrived energetically as usual at 9:30. But this morning, the young lady who was his secretary had arrived with him. Pitcher watched them with interest. Harvey Maxwell didn't pay attention to Pitcher. He said only a quick "Good morning," and ran to his desk. He dug energetically into the mountain of letters and telegrams that waited for him. The stockbroker's day had begun.

2 Miss Leslie, the young lady, had been Maxwell's secretary for a year. She was beautiful, and she dressed simply. Unlike some secretaries, she never wore cheap glass jewelry. Her dress was gray and plain, but it fitted her body nicely. With it she wore a small black hat with a green-gold flower at the side. This morning her face shone with happiness. Her eyes were bright, her face a soft pink.

3 Pitcher, still interested, noticed that she acted differently this morning. Usually she walked straight inside to her own desk. But this morning she stayed in the outside office. She

walked over near Maxwell's desk. Maxwell didn't seem to be a man anymore. He had changed into a busy New York stockbroker. He'd become a machine of many moving parts.

4   "Well—what is it? Is anything wrong?" Maxwell asked his secretary. He wasn't looking at her. His eyes were on his mail. Letters and telegrams lay on his desk like snow.

5   "It's nothing," she said softly. She moved away with a little smile. "Mr. Pitcher," she said, coming over to him, "did Mr. Maxwell ask you to hire another secretary yesterday?"

6   "Yes, he did," answered Pitcher. "He told me to get another one. I asked the secretarial school to send over a few this morning. But it's 9:45, and no one has come yet."

7   "I will do the work as usual, then," said the young lady, "until someone comes to fill the place." And she went to her desk at once. She hung up the black hat with the green-gold flower in its usual place.

8   Harvey Maxwell was always a busy stockbroker, but today he was even busier than usual. The ticker tape machine began to throw out tape. The desk telephone began to ring. Men crowded into the office, buying and selling, crying and yelling. Boys ran in and out with telegrams. Even Pitcher's face looked more alive. Maxwell pushed his chair against the wall. He ran energetically from ticker tape to telephone, jumping like a dancer.

9   In the middle of all this action and yelling, the stockbroker realized that someone new had arrived. He first saw a high mountain of golden hair under a large round hat. Then he noticed some large glass jewelry. Underneath all this was a young lady. Pitcher saw that Maxwell didn't know who she was. He came forward to explain. "Here is the lady from the secretarial school," Pitcher said to Maxwell. "She came for the job."

10   Maxwell turned around with his hands full of papers and ticker tape. "What job?" he yelled. His face looked angry.

11   "The secretarial job," Pitcher said quietly. "You told me yesterday to call the school. I asked them to send one over this morning."

12   "You're losing your mind, Pitcher! Why would I tell you a thing like that? Miss Leslie has worked well for a whole year here. The job is hers while she wants to stay.

There is no job here, Madam! Tell the secretarial school, Pitcher. Don't bring any more of them in here!"

13   The lady turned to leave. Her hat almost hit Pitcher in the eye as she angrily walked past him out of the office. Pitcher thought to himself that Maxwell was getting more forgetful every day.

II

14   The office became busier and busier. Orders to buy and sell came and went like birds flying. Maxwell was worried about his own stocks, too, and worked faster and harder. This was the stock market, the world of money. There was no room in it for the world of human feelings or the world of nature.

15   Near lunchtime, everything quieted down. Maxwell stood by his desk with his hands full of telegrams. His pen was behind his ear. His hair stood up on his head. Suddenly through the open window came a smell of flowers, like the thin breath of spring. Maxwell stood still. This was Miss Leslie's smell, her own and only hers. The smell seemed to bring her before him. The world of the stock market disappeared. And Miss Leslie was in the next room—only twenty steps away.

16   "I'll do it now," said Maxwell softly. "I'll ask her now. Why didn't I do it long ago?"

17   He ran into her office. He jumped towards her desk. She looked up at him with a smile. Her face turned a soft pink. Her eyes were kind. Maxwell put his hands on her desk. They were still full of papers.

18   "Miss Leslie," he said, hurrying, "I only have a moment to talk. I want to say something important in that moment: Will you be my wife? I haven't had time to show you, but I really do love you. Speak quickly please—there's the telephone."

19   "Why—what are you talking about?" cried the young lady. She stood up and looked at him strangely.

20   "Don't you understand?" Maxwell asked quickly, looking back at the phone on his desk. "I want you to marry me. I've stolen this moment to ask you, now, while things have quieted down a little. Take the telephone, Pitcher!" he yelled. "Will you, Miss Leslie?" he added softly.

21   The secretary acted very strange. At first she seemed surprised. Then she began to cry. But then she smiled through her tears like the sun through rain. She put her arm around the stockbroker's neck.

22   "I know now," she said. "It's this business that put it out of your head. I was afraid, at first. But don't you remember, Harvey? We were married last evening at 8:00, in the little church around the corner."

AFTER YOU READ THE STORY

A. Understanding the Plot

Answer the following questions with complete sentences.

1. What is Maxwell's business?
2. Who works with him, and what do they do? In the picture on page 5, which man is Pitcher and which is Maxwell?
3. Why is Pitcher so interested in Maxwell this morning?
4. What telephone call did Pitcher make for Maxwell yesterday? Why?
5. What question does Maxwell ask Miss Leslie?
6. Why is she so surprised?

B. Close Reading

Below are some statements about Part I of "The Romance of a Busy Broker." If the statement is true, write T beside it. If it is not true, write F for false, and then on a separate piece of paper rewrite the sentence to make it true.

_____ 1. Pitcher was an energetic man, and his feelings could always be seen in his face.

_____ 2. Harvey Maxwell was a man who put great energy into his work.

_____ 3. The young lady with Maxwell seemed unhappy, and she dressed badly.

_____ 4. The young lady asked Pitcher if Maxwell had asked him to get another secretary.

_____ 5. The young lady went to her desk because no one from the secretarial school had arrived.

_____ 6. The office was quiet and peaceful after Maxwell and the young lady began work.

_____ 7. Maxwell told the young lady from the secretarial school that the job was hers if she wanted it.

C. Vocabulary Practice

The paragraph below tells what happened in Part II of the story. Fill in the blanks with words from the following list. The first blank has been filled in for you.

busier	faster	hurry	quieted
business	feelings	married	smiled
church	flowers	marry	stocks
cry	harder	office	tears
~~energetically~~			

After the lady from the secretarial school left, Maxwell returned ___**energetically**___ to his work and became even

_____ than usual. He was worried about his own
                    1

_____, and worked _____ and
          2   3

_____. There was no room for human
          4

_____ in his world of money. But near lunchtime
          5

everything _____ down. Maxwell smelled a smell
                          6

of _____ through the window. It made him think
              7

of Miss Leslie. "I'll do it now," he thought, and went into her

_____. Miss Leslie _____ when she
          8   9

saw him. But Maxwell was in a _____ and spoke
                                              10

fast. "Will you _____ me?" he asked. She was
                          11

angry at first, then she began to _____. But at last
                                                  12

she smiled through her _____. "I know now," she
said. "It's this _____ that put it out of your head.
  14
We were _____ last night at the little
  15
_____ around the corner."
  16

D. Word Forms

In some words, the noun form is the same as the present tense
form of the verb (for example, *surprise* is both a noun form and
a verb form). The past form of such a regular verb *(surprised)* is
also the adjective form.

Teachers often **surprise** (v.) their students with quizzes. The
quizzes are not always a pleasant **surprise** (n.). Some students
are **surprised** (adj.) if they get a good grade.

Put the correct form of the word (noun, verb, or adjective) in the
blank spaces.

1. (*surprise / surprised*) Pitcher, a quiet man, looked

   _____ this morning. The _____ for him

   was the arrival of Harvey Maxwell and his secretary

   together. Maxwell did not usually _____ Pitcher,

   but this was something special.

2. (*interest / interested*) Pitcher, _____ in the young

   lady's actions, watched her carefully. He noticed with

   _____ that she did not walk inside to her own desk

   as usual. Her work usually _____ her, but not

   today, it seemed.

3. (*crowd / crowded*) The office seemed _____ with

   businessmen buying and selling, and boys running in and

   out with telegrams. This kind of _____ came into

   the office every day. They _____ in, talked loudly,

   and interrupted work.

4. (*dress / dressed*) Miss Leslie's _____ was gray and plain and beautiful. Later, another woman came into the office, _____ in bright colors, with cheap jewelry and a large round hat. She would _____ like this for work every day.

5. (*change / changed*) Maxwell _____ into a machine as soon as he entered his office, by digging into a mountain of letters and telegrams. The _____ in the man was complete: He no longer seemed like a man. Was it the thought of money that _____ him so?

E. Language Activity: The New York Stock Exchange

Today, stockbrokers do not use ticker tape machines as they did in the old days. But the buying and selling of stocks has not changed very much. Businessmen and businesswomen still follow the stock market carefully. One way they do this is by reading about stocks every day in the newspaper. Here are some examples from the long list of stocks that are bought and sold on the New York Stock Exchange (or market).

The New York Stock Exchange						
1	2	3	4	5	6	7
52-Week			Yesterday			
High	Low	Stock	High	Low	Last	Change
60.13	32.00	Boeing	60.06	56.94	59.06	+2.29
43.88	23.38	Disney	38.44	37.00	37.19	−1.84
60.50	38.25	GenElec	57.06	55.00	56.63	−0.44
28.63	14.38	Polaroid	15.00	14.25	14.88	+0.31
79.50	35.06	RadioShk	62.25	61.06	62.00	−3.38
108.25	60.75	Toyota	79.13	78.69	78.94	+0.06

Columns 1 and 2 show the high and low price of the stock last year (52 weeks).

Column 3 shows the names of companies that offer stock.

Columns 4 and 5 show the high and low price of the stock during yesterday's trading.

Column 6 shows the price of the stock at the end of the day yesterday.

Column 7 shows the difference in price between the last trade yesterday and the previous day's price.

Working alone, or with another student, find answers to the following questions from the chart on page 10.

1. Which company had the highest price at the end of yesterday's trading? Which had the lowest?
2. Which company had the greatest upward change in its price yesterday? Which had the greatest downward change in price?
3. Which company had the greatest dollar change in its price last year? Which had the smallest?
4. Which company would you like to own stock in, and why?
5. Look at the stock listings in yesterday's newspaper. Find one of the companies listed on page 10. What was its price yesterday? How does that compare with the price on the previous page?
6. Choose one or two stocks from yesterday's newspaper to "buy." Keep that newspaper. After one month, check on your stock(s) in that day's newspaper. Discover whether you would have gained or lost money if you had actually bought that stock.

F. Discussion: How Busy Can Busy Get?

1. Can you remember a time when you were so busy that you forgot something important? What were you doing? What did you forget?
2. Can you remember a time when someone else was so busy that he or she forgot something important about *you*? What was it? How did you feel? What did you do?
3. In "The Romance of a Busy Broker," Harvey Maxwell is so busy that he forgets that he was married "last evening at 8:00, in the little church around the corner." Do you believe this is possible? If so, and if you were the woman, would you act the way Miss Leslie did? If you don't believe it, did you enjoy the story anyway? Why, or why not?

G. Writing: Controlled Composition

Answer the following questions with complete sentences. Make a paragraph of your answers. It will be a summary of "The Romance of a Busy Broker." If there are underlined words in the questions, use them in your answers. The first two have been done for you.

Example: Where did Pitcher work?

> Pitcher worked in the office of Harvey Maxwell, the stockbroker.

What kind of a man was he usually?

> Usually, he was a quiet man.

- Where did Pitcher work?
- What kind of man was he usually?
- But how did he act this morning?
- Why was he interested this morning?
- How did Maxwell usually arrive at the office?
- What did Maxwell do after he said "Good morning"?
- What did Miss Leslie ask Pitcher?
- Then what did she do?
- As the morning passed, how did the office seem, and how did Maxwell act?
- Who came into the office then?
- Why had she come?
- What did Maxwell say to her?
- How did she feel? And what did she do?
- Later, near lunchtime, what happened in the office?
- What did Maxwell suddenly smell?
- What did the smell make Maxwell think of?
- What did he decide to do?
- When he went into Miss Leslie's office, what did he say?
- At first, how did she act?
- What did she understand later?
- What had the busy broker forgotten?

2

THE INGRATE

✳

Adapted from the story by
PAUL LAURENCE DUNBAR

Paul Laurence Dunbar was born in Dayton, Ohio, in 1872. His father had been a slave; he had been owned by a white man in the South. Like Josh, one of the two main characters in "The Ingrate," Dunbar's father escaped to freedom in the North and fought for the North in the Civil War (1861–1865). Dunbar was sickly as a child and spent much of his time alone reading. He began to write as a young man, and at first he published mostly poetry. He earned very little money from his writing, and he was working as an elevator operator when he met the well-known writer and editor William Dean Howells. He took an interest in Dunbar and wrote an introduction to a collection of Dunbar's poetry, *Lyrics of Lowly Life*. This and his later books of poetry made Dunbar well known as a poet during his lifetime. Now, his novels and stories are better known than his poetry. Dunbar died in Dayton in 1906, at the age of only thirty-four.

BEFORE YOU READ THE STORY

A. About the Author

Read the paragraph about Paul Laurence Dunbar on page 13. What important information does the paragraph tell you about Dunbar's father? During his lifetime, was Dunbar better known for his poetry or for his stories and novels?

B. The Pictures

1. In the picture on page 18, there are at least two important differences between the two men in the picture. What are they? Can you think of other differences?
2. Look at the picture on page 21. What do you think is happening here? Why?

C. Thinking About Slavery and Freedom

1. A slave is someone whose life and work are under the control of another, the owner or master. Most of us have a sense of what freedom is; but few living people have experienced slavery, the complete opposite of freedom. Slavery was common in ancient times. It existed in the United States until the end of the Civil War. Do you think it continues to exist anywhere, or in any form, today in the twenty-first century?
2. When do you feel most free? Why? When do you feel least free? Why? Is it possible to be a slave to a thing or an idea as well as to another person? If so, when, or under what conditions? If not, why not?

D. Scanning for Information

Quickly scan the Key Words paragraph on page 15 to find three important facts about the story. Try to answer the three questions below in less than five minutes.

1. What does the story's title mean?
2. What are the names of the two main characters in the story?
3. What sort of a group were the Quakers?

An **ingrate** is a person who shows no **gratitude,** who gives no thanks for help or kindness shown to him or her. Dunbar's story has two main characters: One is Mr. Leckler, a white farmer who owns a large **plantation** in the South with its many fields, buildings, and animals. Mr. Leckler believes he is a man of strong **principles,** deep and proper beliefs about what is right and wrong. The other main character is Josh, a black slave who is owned by Leckler. There are also some **abolitionists** in the story, that is, people who wanted to end (abolish) slavery completely. Many abolitionists belonged to a religious group called **Quakers.**

THE INGRATE

I

Mr. Leckler was a man of high principle. He had often said this to Mrs. Leckler. She was often called in to listen to him. Mr. Leckler was one of those people with an endless hunger for advice, though he never acted on it. Mrs. Leckler knew this, but like a good little wife, she always offered him her little gifts of advice. Today, her husband's mind was troubled—as usual, troubled about a question of principle.

2   "Mrs. Leckler," he said, "I am troubled in my mind. I'm troubled by a question of principle."

3   "Yes, Mr. Leckler?" his wife asked.

4   "If I were a cheating northern Yankee, I would be rich now. But I am too honest and generous. I always let my principles get between me and my duty." Mr. Leckler was sure of his own goodness. "Now, here is the question that troubles my principles. My slave, Josh, has been working for Mr. Eckley in Lexington. I think that city cheat has been dishonest. He lied about how many hours Josh worked, and cut down his pay for it. Now, of course, *I* don't care, the question of a dollar or two is nothing to *me*. But it's a

different question for poor Josh." Mr. Leckler's voice became sadder. "You know, Josh wants to buy his freedom from me. And I generously give him part of what he earns. Every dollar Mr. Eckley cheats him of cuts down his pay and puts farther away his hopes of freedom."

5   Mrs. Leckler knew that Mr. Leckler let Josh keep only one-tenth of what he earned for extra work. So Mr. Eckley's dishonesty hurt her husband more than it hurt Josh. But she didn't say anything about that. She only asked, "But what troubles you about duty and principle here, Mr. Leckler?"

6   Mr. Leckler answered, "Well, if Josh knew how to read and write and do numbers . . ."

7   "Mr. Leckler, are you crazy!" she cried.

8   "Listen to me, my dear, and give me your advice. This is an important question. If Josh knew these things he wouldn't be cheated when he worked away from me."

9   "But teaching a slave . . ."

10   "Yes, Mrs. Leckler, that's what troubles me. I know my duty—I know what the law and other people say about teaching a slave. But it is against my principles that that poor black man is being cheated. Really, Mrs. Leckler, I think I may teach him secretly, so he can defend himself."

11   "Well, of course," said Mrs. Leckler, "do what you think is best."

12   "I knew you would agree with me," he answered. "I'm glad to have your advice, my dear." And so this master of principle walked out to see his valuable slave. He was very pleased with his generosity. "I'll get Eckley next time!" he said to himself.

13   Josh, the subject of Mr. Leckler's principles, worked as a plasterer on Mr. Leckler's plantation, working on the walls and ceilings of the plantation's many buildings. Josh was very good at his work, and other men wanted him to work for them, too. So Mr. Leckler made money by letting Josh work on their plantations in his free time. Josh was a man of high intelligence. When he asked Mr. Leckler if he could buy his freedom with the money he made on other plantations, Mr. Leckler quickly agreed. He knew he could let his valuable slave keep only a little of the money he earned. Most of what Josh earned would belong to his master. Of course, Mr. Leckler knew that when the black man learned his numbers things would change. But it would be years

before Josh could earn $2,000, the price Mr. Leckler asked for Josh's freedom. And, Mr. Leckler thought, by the time Josh came close to earning the money, the cost of a slave's freedom might suddenly go higher.

14 When Josh heard his master's plan, his eyes shone with pleasure, and he worked even harder than before. Even Mr. Leckler, who knew his plasterer's intelligence, was surprised how quickly Josh was learning to read, write, and figure. Mr. Leckler didn't know that on one of Josh's work trips a freed slave had given Josh some lessons. Josh already knew the beginnings of how to read before he began his lessons with Mr. Leckler. But he certainly wasn't going to tell Mr. Leckler that.

15 So a year passed away, and Mr. Leckler thought Josh had learned enough.

16 "You know, Josh," he said, "I have already gone against my principles and disobeyed the law for you. A man can't go against his principles too far, even for someone who is being cheated. I think you can take care of yourself now."

17 "Oh, yes, sir, I guess I can," said Josh.

18 "And you shouldn't be seen with any books, now."

19 "Oh, no, sir, certainly not," Josh said obediently. He certainly didn't plan to be seen with any books.

20 Just now, Mr. Leckler saw the good in what he had done. His heart was full of a great joy. Mr. Eckley was building on to his house, and asked Josh to do the plastering. When the job was done, Josh figured that Eckley had cheated him again. Eckley was very surprised when the black man looked at the numbers and showed him his dishonesty, but he passed him the two dollars. "Leckler did this," Mr. Eckley thought to himself. "Teaching a black his numbers! Leckler just wanted more money for himself! I should call the law!"

21 Mr. Leckler was very pleased when he heard that Josh had caught Eckley cheating. He said to himself, "Ha! I caught him, the old thief!" But to Mrs. Leckler he said, "You see, my dear, my craziness in teaching Josh was right. See how much money he saved for himself."

22 "What did he save?" asked the little wife without thinking.

23 Her husband turned red, and then answered, "Well, of course it was only 20 cents saved for *him*, but to a slave

buying his freedom, every cent counts. It is not the money, Mrs. Leckler, it's the principle of the thing."

24   "Yes," said the lady obediently.

II

25   It is easy enough for the master to order the body of a slave, "This far you may go, and no further." The master has laws and chains to hold the slave back. But what master can say to the mind of a slave, "I order you to stop learning"? Josh had begun to eat the forbidden fruit of learning, and he was hungry for more. Night after night he sat by his lonely fire and read one of his few books. Other slaves laughed at him. They told him to get a wife. But Josh had no time for love or marriage. He had other hopes than to have his children be slaves to Mr. Leckler. To him, slavery was the dark night in which he dreamed of freedom. His dream was to own himself—to be the master of his own hands and feet, of his whole body. When he thought of this, something would catch at his heart, and his breath came hard between his lips. But he was quiet and obedient before his master, and Mr. Leckler was pleased. Usually intelligence in a slave meant trouble. But who seemed more untroubled than Josh? Mr. Leckler said to his wife,

26   "You see, my dear, it's important to do the right thing, even to a black."

27   All this time, the white hills of the Yankee North seemed to call to Josh. The north wind told him that in the North he would be a slave no longer. Josh knew it would be hard to win his freedom. Worst of all was the law. It stood like a stone wall between slavery and freedom, between slavery and Josh's hopes. Then one day, when he was working away from home, a voice called to him from the woods, "Be brave!" And later that night the voice called to him like the north wind, "Follow."

28   "It seems to me that Josh should have come home tonight," said Mr. Leckler. "But maybe he got through too late to catch a train." In the morning he said, "Well, he's not here yet. He must have to do some extra work. If he doesn't get home tonight, I'll go up there."

29   That night he did take the train to where Josh had been working. He learned that Josh had left the night before. But where could he have gone? For the first time, Mr. Leckler

realized that Josh had run away. Mr. Leckler was very angry. He knew that the most valuable slave on his plantation was going north to freedom. He walked the floor all night, but he couldn't go after Josh until morning.

30   Early the next day, he put the dogs on Josh's trail. The dogs followed it into the woods, but in a few minutes they came back, crying and lost. Josh had played an old slave trick—he had put hot pepper in his footprints. Finally the dogs found Josh's trail further in the woods. Leckler followed the trail until he came to a train station about six miles away. Mr. Leckler asked the stationmaster if he had seen a black get on the train.

31   "Yes," the man said, "two nights ago."

32   "But why did you let him go without a pass?" cried Mr. Leckler in anger.

33   "I didn't," said the stationmaster. "He had a written pass signed 'James Leckler.'"

34   "Lies, lies!" cried Mr. Leckler. "He wrote it himself!"

35   "Well, how could I know?" answered the stationmaster. "Our blacks around here don't know how to write."

36   Mr. Leckler suddenly decided to keep quiet. Josh was probably in the arms of some Yankee abolitionist by now. There was nothing to do but put up advertisements for Josh's return. He went home and spoke angrily to his wife.

37   "You see, Mrs. Leckler, this is what comes of my generous heart. I taught a black to read and write. Now look how he uses this knowledge. Oh, the ingrate, the ingrate! He turns against me the weapon I gave him to defend himself! Here's the most valuable slave on my plantation gone—gone, I tell you—and all because of my kindness. It isn't his *value* I'm thinking about. It's the *principle* of the thing—the ingratitude he has shown me. Oh, if I ever catch him—!"

38   Just at this time, Josh was six miles north of the Ohio River. A kind Quaker was saying softly to Josh, "Lie quiet. You will be safe here. Here comes a slave-catcher, but I know him. I'll talk to him and send him away. You must not fear. None of your brothers and sisters who came to us have ever been taken back to slavery." Then he spoke to the slave-catcher. "Oh, good evening, my friend!" Josh could hear them talking as he hid in a bag among other bags of corn and potatoes.

39   It was after ten o'clock that night when Josh's bag was thrown into a wagon and driven away to the next helping hands. And in this way, hiding by day and traveling by night, Josh went north. He was helped all along the way by a few of his own people who had been freed, and always by the good Quakers. And so he made his way to Canada. And on one never-to-be-forgotten morning he stood up straight, breathed God's air, and knew himself free!

III

40   To Joshua Leckler, as now he was called, this life in Canada was all new and strange. It was a new thing for him to feel that he was a man like any other man he met among the whites. It was new, too, to be paid what his work was worth. He worked more happily than he had ever done. He was even pleased at how tired his work made him feel.

41   Sometimes there came to his ears stories of his brothers and sisters in the South. Often he met escaped slaves like himself. Their sad stories made him burn to do something to help people he had left behind him. But these escaped slaves, and the newspapers he read, told him other things, too. They said that the idea of freedom was rising in the United States. Already, people were speaking out about abolishing slavery and freeing the slaves. Already people were helping those abolitionist leaders like Sumner, Phillips, Douglass, Garrison. Joshua heard the names Lucretia Mott and Harriet Beecher Stowe. And Joshua was hopeful, for after the long night of slavery he saw the first light of morning.

42   So the years passed. Then from those dark clouds of slavery the storm of war broke: the thunder of guns and the rain of bullets. From his home in the North Joshua watched the storm. Sometimes the war went well for the North, sometimes for the South. Then suddenly out from the storm came a cry like the voice of God, "You and your brothers and sisters are free!" Free, free, with freedom for all—not just for a few. Freedom for all who had been enslaved. Not free by escaping in the night—free to live in the light of morning.

43   When the northern army first called for black soldiers, Joshua went to Boston to sign up. Since he could read and write, and because of his general intelligence, he was soon

made an officer. One day Mr. Leckler saw a list of names of these black soldiers. His eyes stopped at the name "Joshua Leckler." He showed the list to Mrs. Leckler.

44   "Mrs. Leckler," he said, "look what happened because I taught a black to read and write. I disobeyed the law of my state. I lost my slave. And I gave the Yankees a smart officer to help them fight the war. I was wrong—I was wrong. But I am right, too, Mrs. Leckler. This all happened because of my generous heart, and your bad advice. But oh, that ingrate, that ingrate!"

AFTER YOU READ THE STORY

A. Understanding the Plot

Answer the following questions with complete sentences.

1. What work did Josh do on Mr. Leckler's plantation?
2. Why did Mr. Leckler let Josh work on other plantations, too?
3. Why was Josh trying to save money?
4. How did Josh escape, and where did he go?
5. What happened in the United States that made Josh want to join the northern army?
6. What did Josh become in the army? How did Mr. Leckler find out what Josh had done?

B. Close Reading

Part I (pages 15–19)
Mr. Leckler's real reasons for doing a thing are often different from the reasons he gives to his wife or Josh. By answering the following questions, you will explore and explain these differences. Paragraph numbers are given to help you find the correct answers.

1. What reason does Mr. Leckler give for being troubled in his mind? (paragraph 2)
2. What reason does Mr. Leckler give for being angry with Mr. Eckley? (paragraph 4)
3. What reasons does Mr. Leckler give for teaching Josh to read and do numbers? (paragraphs 8, 10)

4. But what is Mr. Leckler's real reason for being troubled, for being angry, and for wanting to teach Josh to read and do numbers? (paragraph 5)
5. What reason does Mr. Leckler give for allowing Josh to keep part of what he earns working for other slave owners? (paragraph 4)
6. But what is Mr. Leckler's real reason for agreeing to let Josh buy his freedom with the money he earns? (paragraph 13)

Parts II and III (pages 19–23)

Complete the following sentences. Make sure that the whole sentence, not just part of it, is true.

1. Josh decided to escape from Mr. Leckler and slavery because
   a. he had no time for love or marriage.
   b. other slaves laughed at him for learning to read.
   c. slavery was the dark night in which he dreamed of freedom.

2. Mr. Leckler put dogs on Josh's trail, and at first
   a. they found Josh's trail further in the woods.
   b. they were confused by the pepper Josh put in his footprints.
   c. they followed the trail to a train station about six miles away.

3. Josh was able to escape from Mr. Leckler and the South
   a. with the help of Quaker abolitionists and other freed slaves.
   b. as soon as he learned to write a train pass.
   c. because Mr. Leckler had let him earn some money of his own.

4. Josh was happier living and working in the North
   a. when war broke out in the South.
   b. after he joined the northern army.
   c. because he could live and work freely like anyone else.

5. Josh went to Boston to sign up for the army
   a. because he could read and write.
   b. as soon as the northern army called for black soldiers.
   c. when they made him an officer.

C. Vocabulary Practice

Words that are opposite in meaning are called *antonyms* (examples: *true* and *false*, *right* and *wrong*, *good* and *bad*). Many adjective antonyms can be made by adding the prefix *un-* or *dis-* to the word. Look at the following words from the story and their *antonyms*:

generous—ungenerous   honest—dishonest
grateful—ungrateful   obedient—disobedient
troubled—untroubled

Complete the following sentences with the correct pair of antonyms.

1. Mr. Leckler tells his wife that Mr. Eckley is _____ because he has cheated Josh. But we understand that Mr. Leckler himself is not always _____.

2. Mr. Leckler tells his wife how _____ he is because he lets Josh earn his own money. Mrs. Leckler never tells her husband that in fact he is _____ because he lets Josh keep only one-tenth of what he earns.

3. Mr. Leckler says he is _____ because of his "principles." But he seems completely _____ about increasing the cost of Josh's freedom when Josh would come close to earning the $2,000.

4. Josh always acts _____ toward his master; he does what Mr. Leckler tells him to do. We understand how _____ Josh has really been in his heart when he escapes from slavery.

5. In the end, Mr. Leckler thinks that Josh should have been _____ for the help he received in learning to read. In fact, he was so _____ that he ran away!

D. Word Forms

Word Forms on page 9 uses words that have the same form for both noun and verb. Some examples of such words from "The Ingrate" are *value* (n.)—*value* (v.) and *trail* (n.)—*trail* (v.). Usually, however, the noun form of a word is different from the verb form. This exercise asks you to decide which form to use in a sentence.

Put the correct form of the word (noun or verb) in the blank spaces in each sentence. All the verb forms should be in the past tense.

1. (*advice / advise*) Mr. Leckler's wife always _____ him, when he asked her. But he never acted on the _____ she gave him.

2. (*earnings / earn*) Mr. Leckler let Josh keep some of what he _____ from working for other slave owners. The idea was that these _____ would some day buy him his freedom.

3. (*teaching / teach*) Mr. Leckler _____ Josh to read and do numbers even though his neighbors believed that only disobedience and trouble would result from such _____.

4. (*building / build*) Mr. Eckley added a new part to his house and hired Josh to plaster the walls of the _____ he had _____.

5. (*obedience / obey*) Mr. Leckler expected _____ from both his wife and Josh, but in the end it was only his wife who _____ him.

6. (*cheating / cheat*) Mr. Eckley's _____ was seen very quickly by Mr. Leckler; the way Mr. Leckler himself _____ Josh, however, was less easy for the world to see.

E. Language Activity: Abolitionists

Paragraph 41 gives the names of some famous abolitionists, the people who led the effort to free the slaves. Their full names are:

Frederick Douglass   William Lloyd Garrison   Lucretia Mott
Wendell Phillips   Harriet Beecher Stowe   Charles Sumner

Working with a partner if possible, choose one of the people listed above and look in an encyclopedia to find information about him or her. You may not understand everything written in the encyclopedia, but you should be able to find answers to many of the following questions. Be prepared to report the information you find to the class.

- Where and when was this person born?
- What kind of family did this person grow up in?
- What can you find out about this person's education?
- What work did he or she do?
- What was this person's importance to the work for abolition?
- What is this person most famous for?
- When and where did this person die?

F. Discussion: "A Question of Principle"

1. Mr. Leckler talks a lot about his principles:

   I'm troubled by a question of principle. (paragraph 2)

   I always let my principles get between me and my duty. (paragraph 4)

   But it is against my principles that that poor black man is being cheated. (paragraph 10)

   I have already gone against my principles and disobeyed the law for you. (paragraph 16)

   It is not the money, Mrs. Leckler, it's the principle of the thing. (paragraph 23)

   When Mr. Leckler says that it is against his principles that a slave is being cheated, what principles does he mean? When he tells Josh that he has gone against his principles in teaching him to read and do numbers, what principles does he mean? What "principles" actually seem to govern or control his behavior? Does Dunbar consider Leckler a "man of high principle"?

2. What are some principles that you believe in strongly? Is it difficult to hold and follow those principles? Why, or why not?

G. Writing: A Speech to the Abolitionists

Imagine that you are Josh. The Civil War has just begun. You have been asked to give a short speech in Boston at a meeting of people who work to abolish slavery. Write your speech. Begin:

Ladies and Gentlemen, Brothers and Sisters:
My name is Joshua Leckler, and I have escaped from slavery.

In telling your audience about your life and experience, be sure to include answers to the following questions. Paragraph numbers are given to guide you in case you want help from the story.

- What was the name of the man who called himself your master? (paragraph 33)
- What work did you do on his plantation? Why did you also do this work for other slave owners? How much of this money were you allowed to keep for yourself? What did you plan to do with the money you saved? (paragraphs 5, 13)
- Why did Mr. Leckler decide to help you learn to read and do numbers? What did you think this education might mean to you? (paragraphs 10, 13, 31–34)
- How did you escape from Mr. Leckler? Where did you go? Who helped you escape? (paragraphs 30–39)
- How did it feel to be free? What was new and different in your life? (paragraph 40)
- Why have you come to Boston now? (paragraph 43)
- What are you most worried about at this moment in your life? What are you most grateful for?
- What promise do you make to your audience about fighting for freedom?

3

HOW I WENT TO THE MINES

Adapted from the story by
BRET HARTE

Bret Harte was born in Albany, New York, in 1836. His father was a schoolteacher who died young. His mother remarried and moved to San Francisco. When Harte was seventeen, he moved there to join his mother and her second husband. In California, Harte turned to journalism and short story writing after trying several other jobs. For a while he was an unsuccessful gold miner. His story "How I Went to the Mines" came from that experience. In 1868, he became the first editor of the magazine *Overland Monthly*. In the same year he published a story, "The Luck of Roaring Camp," that brought him national fame. Harte is generally considered to be the first American writer of stories of "local color"—that is, stories about a special place, its people, and its way of life. When his stories about the West made him famous, he went East to write for the *Atlantic Monthly* for $10,000 a year (a very large amount in those days). But neither this success nor his popularity as a writer lasted long. As a result, he left the United States in 1877 to work as a businessman and U.S. consul in Europe. He finally settled in England in 1885, where he lived and continued to publish books until his death in 1902.

BEFORE YOU READ THE STORY

A. About the Author

Read the paragraph on page 29. For what kind of writing is Bret Harte best known? Why did he move to Europe? How long did he live there?

B. The Pictures

1. Look at the picture on page 35. What sort of place is this? What do you think is happening here?
2. On page 38, the same young man is showing something to another man. What might it be? How would you describe the expressions on their faces?

C. Thinking About the Gold Rush

In 1848–1849 gold was discovered in California, and many people rushed there to dig for it, hoping to become rich. If you had lived at that time, would you have wanted to join the "gold rush"? Why, or why not? Today, are there jobs, fields of work, or parts of the world that seem to promise that a person can "get rich quick"? What or where are they? Are you interested in these jobs or places?

D. Skimming to Get an Impression

Sometimes we want to get a general idea, or impression, of a piece of writing before we read it carefully. To do this, we read quickly over the material. We don't try to understand details.

Skim Part I of "How I Went to the Mines." Read the first two sentences of each paragraph, then answer as many of the following questions as you can *without looking back at Part I*. Answer the questions in no more than five minutes. Then check your answers by reading Part I carefully.

1. Where does the story take place?
2. What was the young man's profession or job?
3. Where did he decide to go? Why?
4. Where did he sleep while he traveled?
5. Was he delighted or disappointed when he got to where he was going?

Mines are places under the earth from which gold, metals, and precious stones are taken. A white stone called **quartz** at the surface often points the way to gold underground. In early times, miners dug for gold with a **pick**, a tool with a sharp metal point that broke the ground, and a **shovel** to lift the dirt into a **pan**, a container that was quite large but not very deep. The dirt was washed away with running water in the pan, leaving **nuggets**—small gold pieces—behind. Miners often worked with one or more **partners**, other men who could help them mine a large area. The area they mined was their **claim**; they marked it with a sign and listed it in a government office. The miners were among the **pioneers**, the people who first settled the West in the United States.

HOW I WENT TO THE MINES

I

I had been in California for two years before I thought of going to the mines. My introduction to gold digging was partly forced on me. I was the somewhat youthful and, I fear, not very experienced schoolmaster of a small pioneer settlement. Our school was only partly paid for by the state; most of the cost was carried by a few families in the settlement. When two families—and about a dozen children—moved away to a richer and newer district, the school was immediately closed.

2   In twenty-four hours, I was without both students and employment. I am afraid I missed the children the most: I had made companions and friends of some of them. I stood that bright May morning before an empty schoolhouse in the wild woods. I felt strange to think that our little summer "play" at being schoolmaster and student was over. I remember clearly a parting gift from a student a year older than I. He gave me a huge piece of gingerbread. It helped me greatly in my journeys, for I was alone in the world at that moment, and by nature extravagant with money.

3   I had been frightfully extravagant even on my small schoolmaster's pay. I had spent much money on fine shirts. I gave as an excuse that I should set an example in dress for my students. The result, however, was that at this important moment, I had only seven dollars in my pocket. I spent five on a second-hand revolver that I felt was necessary to show that I was leaving peaceful employment for one of risk and adventure.

4   For I had finally decided to go to the mines and become a gold digger. Other employment, and my few friends in San Francisco, were expensively distant. The nearest mining district was only forty miles away. My hope was that when I got there I would find a miner named Jim I had met once in San Francisco. With only his name to help me, I expected to find him somewhere in the mines. But my remaining two dollars was not enough for travel by horse and wagon. I must walk to the mines, and I did.

5   I cannot clearly remember *how* I did it. The end of the first day found me with painfully blistered feet. I realized that the shiny leather shoes, so proper for a schoolmaster, were not suited to my wanderings. But I held on to them as a sign of my past life. I carried them in my hands when pain and pride caused me to leave the highway and travel barefoot on the trails.

6   I'm afraid all my belongings looked unsuitable. The few travelers I met on the road looked at me and tried not to smile. I had a fine old leather bag my mother had given me, and a silver-handled whip—also a gift. These did not exactly suit the rough blue blanket and tin coffee pot I carried with them. To my embarrassment, my revolver would not stay properly in its holster at my side. It kept working its way around to where it hung down in front.

7   I was too proud to arrive at Jim's door penniless, so I didn't stop at any hotels along the way. I ate my gingerbread and camped out in the woods. The loneliness I felt once or twice along the road completely disappeared in the sweet and silent companionship of the woods. I wasn't aware of hunger, and I slept soundly, quite forgetting the pain of my blistered feet. In the morning I found I had emptied my water bottle. I also found I had completely overlooked the first rule of camping—to settle near water. But I chewed some unboiled coffee beans for breakfast, and again took up the trail.

8 The pine-filled air, the distant view of mountains, led me onward. I was excited to see strange, white pieces of rock, shining like teeth against the red dirt. This was called *quartz*, I had been told. Quartz was a sign of a gold mining district. At about sunset I came out of the pines and looked across at a mountain side covered with white tents. They stuck up out of the earth like the white quartz. It was the "diggings"!

9 I do not know what I had expected, but I was disappointed. As I looked across at the mining camp, the sun set. A great shadow covered the tents, and a number of tiny lights, like stars, shone in their place. A cold wind rushed down the mountainside. I felt cold in my clothes, wet from a long day's journey. It was nine o'clock when I reached the mining camp. I had been on my feet since sunrise. But I hid my belongings in the bushes, and washed my feet in a stream of water. I put on my terrible leather shoes and limped, in my painful pride, to the first miner's log cabin. Here I learned that Jim was one of four partners who worked a claim two miles away, on the other side of the mountain. There was nothing for me to do but go on. I would find the Magnolia Hotel. I would buy the cheapest food, rest an hour, and then limp painfully, as best I could, to Jim's claim.

II

10 The Magnolia Hotel was a large wooden building. The greater part was given over to a huge drinking saloon. Shining mirrors hung on the walls, and a long bar ran down one side of the room. In the unimportant dining room I ordered fish-balls and coffee because they were cheap and quick. The waiter told me that my friend Jim might live in the settlement. The barkeeper, though, knew everything and everybody, and would tell me the shortest way to his log cabin.

11 I was very tired. I'm afraid I took a longer time over my food than was proper. Then I went into the saloon. It was crowded with miners and traders and a few well-dressed businessmen. Here again my pride led me to extravagance. I was ashamed to ask the important, white-shirted and diamond-pinned barkeeper for information, without buying a drink. I'm afraid I laid down another quarter on the bar. I asked my question, and the barkeeper passed me a bottle

and glass. Suddenly a strange thing happened. As it had some effect on my future, I will tell you about it here.

12   The ceiling of the saloon was held up by a half-dozen tall wooden posts. They stood in front of the bar, about two feet from it. The front of the bar was crowded with drinkers. Suddenly, to my surprise, they all put down their glasses and hurriedly backed into the spaces behind the posts. At the same moment a shot was fired through the large open doors that opened into the saloon.

13   The bullet hit the bar and broke off pieces of wood. The shot was returned from the upper end of the bar. And then for the first time I realized that two men with revolvers were shooting at each other across the saloon.

14   The other men were hiding behind the posts; the barkeeper was down behind the bar. Six shots were fired by the revolvers. As far as I could see nobody was hurt. A mirror was broken, and my glass had been hit by the third shot. But the whole thing passed so quickly, and I was so surprised by it all, that I cannot remember feeling afraid. My only worry was that I would show to the others my youth, inexperience, or shock. I think any shy, proud young man will understand this, and would probably feel as I did. So strong was this feeling that while the smell of the gunpowder was still in my nose, I spoke out. I picked up the broken glass, and said to the barkeeper slowly, coolly, "Will you please fill me another glass? It's not my fault if this one was broken."

15   The barkeeper stood up behind the bar. His face was red and excited. He gave me a strange smile and passed me the bottle and a fresh glass. I heard a laugh behind me, and was embarrassed. I took a large gulp of the fiery drink and hurried to leave. But my blistered feet hurt, and I could only limp to the door. I felt a hand on my back. A voice said quickly, "You're not hurt, old man?" I recognized the man who had laughed. My face felt hot and red. I answered quickly that my feet were blistered from a long walk. I was in a hurry to get to Jim's claim.

16   "Hold on," said the stranger. He went out to the street and called to a man in a horse and wagon. "Drop him," he said, pointing at me, "at Jim's cabin, and then come back here." Then he helped me into the wagon. He slapped me on the back, and said mysteriously, "You'll do!" Then he returned quickly to the saloon.

17   I learned from the driver about the gun fight. Two men had had a wild argument the week before. They had sworn to shoot each other "on sight"—that is, at their next meeting. They were going around with revolvers ready. The driver added that the men seemed to be "pretty bad shooters." And I, knowing nothing of these deadly weapons, and thinking pretty much what he thought, agreed! I said nothing of my own feelings, though, and soon forgot them. For as we came near to Jim's log cabin, I had reached the end of my journey.

III

18   Now, for the first time I began to have doubts about my plan: to ask help and advice from a man I hardly knew. I believe it is a common experience of youth that during the journey I had never felt doubts. But *now*, as I arrived, my youth and inexperience came to me like a shock. And it was followed by a greater one. When at last I left my driver and entered the small log cabin, Jim's partners told me that he had left the partnership and gone back to San Francisco.

19   Perhaps I looked tired and disappointed. One of the partners pulled out the only chair and offered me a drink. With encouragement, I limped through my story. I think I told the exact truth. I was even too tired to make it sound as if Jim and I were really friends.

20   They listened without speaking. Probably they had heard such stories before. I expect they had gone through a harder experience than mine. Then something happened that I am sure could have happened only in California in that time of simplicity and confidence. Without a word of discussion among themselves, without a word to ask about my character or experience, they offered me Jim's partnership, "to try."

21   I went to bed that night in Jim's bunk bed. I was one-fourth owner of a log cabin and a claim I knew nothing about. I looked around me at the four bearded faces, only a few years older than I. I wondered if we were playing at being miners as I had played at being a schoolmaster.

22   I awoke late the next morning and stared around the empty cabin. I could hardly believe that what had happened the night before wasn't a dream. The cabin was made of pine logs with four bunk beds on two sides. Bright sunlight

streamed in through *holes* in the walls. There was a table and chair, and three old boxes for furniture. There was one window beside the open door, and a fireplace at the other end. I was wondering if I had moved into an empty cabin, when my partners entered. They had let me sleep—It was twelve o'clock! My breakfast was ready. They had something funny to tell me—I was a hero!

23   My behavior during the shooting match at the Magnolia saloon was being discussed and reported by men who had been there. The story was wildly enlarged. They said I had stood coolly at the bar, quietly demanding a drink while the shots were being fired! I told my partners the truth, but I am afraid they didn't believe me. They thought I was young enough to be embarrassed by being noticed, and they changed the subject.

24   Yes, they said, I could go digging that day. Where? Oh, anywhere on ground that was not already claimed. There were hundreds of square miles to choose from. How to do it? You mean, you have never mined before? Never dug for gold at all? Never! I saw them look quickly at each other. My heart sank. But I noticed that their eyes were bright and happy. Then I learned that my inexperience was considered lucky. Gold miners believed in "beginner's luck," the unexplained luck that came to first-time miners. But I must choose a place to dig myself, to make the luck work.

25   I was given a pick and shovel, and a pan to wash the gold nuggets from the dirt. I decided to dig on a grassy hillside about two hundred yards from the cabin. They told me to fill my pan with dirt around a large area. In one or two shovels-full I dug up some pieces of shining quartz, and put them hopefully in my pocket. Then I filled my pan. I carried it with difficulty—it was surprisingly heavy—to the stream to wash it. As I moved the pan back and forth in the running water, the red dirt washed away. Only stones and black sand were left. I picked out the stones with my fingers, and kept only a small flat, pretty, round stone. It looked like a coin. I put it in my pocket with the quartz. Then I washed away the black sand. You can imagine how I felt when I saw a dozen tiny gold stars in the bottom of the pan! They were so small that I was afraid I would wash them away. I learned later that they are so heavy that there is very little danger of that. I ran happily to where my partners were working.

26   "Yes, he's got the 'color,' " one said without excitement. "I knew it."

27   I was disappointed. "Then I haven't struck gold?" I said shyly.

28   "Not in *this* pan. You've only got a quarter of a dollar there. But," he continued with a smile, "you only have to get that much in four pans, and you've made enough for your daily food."

29   "And that's all any of us—or anyone on this claim—have made in the last six months!" another partner said.

30   This was another shock to me. But he spoke with good humor and youthful carelessness. I took comfort from that. But I was still disappointed by my first try. I shyly pulled the quartz out of my pocket.

31   "I found these," I said. "They look as if they have gold in them. See how it shines?"

32   My partner smiled. "That's worthless. Those are iron pyrites, called 'fool's gold.' But what's that?" he added quickly. He took the round flat stone from my hand, "Where did you find that?"

33   "In the same hole as the quartz. Is it good for anything?"

34   He did not answer, but turning to the other partners who were coming over to see, he said, "Look!"

35   He laid my stone on another stone and hit it with his pick. I was surprised that it didn't break. Where the pick had hit it, it showed a bright yellow star!

36   I had no time, or need, to ask another question. "Write out a claim notice!" he said to one partner. And, "Run, get a post!" to the other. We put the notice on the post, to announce our claim, and began to dig madly.

37   The gold nugget I had picked up was worth about twelve dollars. We carried many pans, we worked that day and the next hopefully, happily, and without tiring. Then we worked at the claim daily, carefully, and regularly for three weeks. Sometimes we found the "color," and sometimes we didn't. But we nearly always got enough for our daily food. We laughed, joked, told stories and enjoyed ourselves as if we were at an endless picnic. But that twelve-dollar nugget was the first and last find we made on the new, "Beginner's Luck" claim!

AFTER YOU READ THE STORY

A. Understanding the Plot

Answer the following questions using complete sentences.

1. As the story opens, what is the young man doing in California? Why does he leave this job?
2. What does he decide to do next, and where? Who does he hope to find there?
3. How does he travel, and why does he travel that way?
4. What surprising event happens in the saloon?
5. What does he discover about Jim when he reaches his claim? What do Jim's partners offer him?
6. What happens when the young man first digs for gold? What happens after that?

B. Close Reading

Part I (pages 31–33)
In Part I, we are told several things that seemed normal to the young man at the time but might surprise us now. Answer the following questions to show your understanding of these "quiet surprises."

1. Today, we expect the state to pay all major costs of schooling for our children. What in the story tells us that this practice did not exist in California at the time of the story?
2. What do we expect the age difference to be between a teacher and a student in school? What was the age difference between the young schoolmaster and at least one of his students?
3. What sort of gift might we expect a student to give to his or her teacher? What did the young schoolmaster receive from a student? Why did this gift become important to him?
4. At the beginning of his new life and a long journey, the young man had a total of seven dollars. What might we expect him to do with most of it? What in fact did he spend most of it on?

Part II (pages 33–36)
Choose the one sentence or phrase after each statement on page 41 that best shows the young man's lack of experience.

1. He buys a drink in the saloon.
   a. He does it from pride, not because he wants the drink.
   b. He's afraid that the drink costs a quarter.
   c. He feels that his bad dinner should be followed by a good drink.

2. When the gunfight breaks out and all the men in the saloon hide, the young man stays by the bar
   a. to show his courage.
   b. waiting calmly for the barkeeper to answer the question he has asked.
   c. because, unlike the others, he had no idea what was happening.

3. During and just after the gunfight, the young man worries mostly that
   a. he might be hurt or even killed by a bullet.
   b. he might do something to show his inexperience.
   c. he might not get either his drink or an answer to his question.

4. After the fight, the stranger slaps the young man on the back and says, "You'll do!"
   a. The young man understands exactly what the stranger means.
   b. The stranger means, "You'll get into trouble if you stay here."
   c. The stranger likes the young man's youth and bravery.

Part III (pages 36–39)
In Part III, Harte gives us many details about gold mining and gold miners. Put a check mark next to all the statements below and on page 43 that are true about gold mining, the gold miners, or the gold miner's life.

1. The miners' cabin
   ____ The cabin had three windows.
   ____ The cabin's walls had holes in them.
   ____ The cabin had a cooking stove but no heat.
   ____ The furniture included three boxes to sit on or eat from.
   ____ The miners made the cabin look like home by putting pictures on the walls.

2. The gold miners of California

_____ showed confidence even in strangers.

_____ could dig for gold on any land that someone else had not claimed.

_____ worked hard, but without much hope.

_____ worked hard, but without much result.

_____ believed that it was not a bad thing to lack gold-mining experience.

3. Mining for gold

_____ Most of the gold could be found in water.

_____ The miners washed the gold to make it shine.

_____ The miners were not excited to find quartz, but they knew that pyrites were valuable.

_____ The miners used their tools in the following order: pick, shovel, pan.

_____ Generally, gold miners couldn't find enough gold to pay for their daily food.

C. Vocabulary Practice

In each of the following quotations, one word is underlined. Notice the way the word is used in the sentence, and notice also the phrases and sentences that come before or after the sentence—that is, the *context* in which the word appears. Then complete the sentence that follows the quotation to show your understanding of the basic meaning of the underlined word.

Example: *I had been in California for two years. . . . I was the somewhat youthful and, I fear, not very <u>experienced</u> schoolmaster of a small pioneer settlement.* (paragraph 1)

He is not very *experienced* at teaching because **he is young and has not taught for many years.**

1. *I was . . . by nature <u>extravagant</u> with money. . . . I had been frightfully extravagant even on my small schoolmaster's pay. I had spent much money on fine shirts.* (paragraphs 2, 3)

The young man shows that he is *extravagant* by _____

_____ .

2. *The end of the first day found me with painfully <u>blistered</u> feet. I realized that the shiny leather shoes, so proper for a schoolmaster, were not suited to my wanderings.* (paragraph 5)

The young man had *blistered* feet because _____

_____.

3. *I put on my terrible leather shoes and <u>limped</u>, in my painful pride, to the first miner's log cabin.* (paragraph 9)

The young man *limped* because _____

_____.

4. *I was <u>ashamed</u> to ask an important, white-shirted and diamond-pinned barkeeper for information, without buying a drink.* (paragraph 11)

The young man would feel *ashamed* to ask his question

unless _____, and this was because _____

_____.

5. *Then something happened that I am sure could have happened only in California in that time of simplicity and <u>confidence</u>.* (paragraph 20)

What did the miners do at that time that showed their

confidence? (You must look back at the text for the answer.)

_____.

D. Word Forms

Choose the correct noun, verb, or adjective form of the word given to complete each sentence. All the verb forms should be in the past tense.

1. (*employment / employ / employed*) A small pioneer school

_____ the young man to teach.

2. (*embarrassment / embarrass / embarrassed*) The young man

was _____ that his revolver would not

stay properly at his side.

3. (*disappointment / disappoint / disappointed*) His first view of the mining camp _____ the young man.

4. (*recognition / recognize / recognized*) The young man's face was hot and red. It showed his _____ of the man who had laughed at him.

5. (*encouragement / encourage / encouraged*) Jim's partners _____ the young man to tell his story.

6. (*confidence / confide / confident*) Jim's partners were _____ that the young man would be a good addition to their partnership.

E. Language Activity: An Improvisation

An *improvisation* is a short play or scene in which the actors do not know exactly what they will say before the scene begins. Each actor chooses a character and decides what sort of a person he or she is. After that, the actors make up what to say and do as the situation develops. With other members of your class, choose one of the following situations. Decide who should play which character. Read the "possible events." Add some of your own. Decide together what, in a general sense, will happen in your scene. Use one area of the classroom as a stage. Write one sentence for one of the actors to begin the action. Then, let the actors say what they want to say and do what they want to do. If two actors speak at the same time, don't stop. Let your words and actions run freely.

Situation 1: In the Classroom

Place: The young man's schoolroom in the pioneer settlement. The young schoolmaster is teaching a lesson in simple mathematics (arithmetic).

Possible Characters: The young man (or woman). A student who is good at math. A student who is not good at math. A student who is sick and wants to go home. A student who behaves badly. A student who is older than the teacher but in love with him or her. A pioneer parent.

Possible Events: The teacher is teaching multiplication and/or division. Sometime during the lesson, the pioneer parent enters the schoolroom with an important message.

Situation 2: At the Magnolia Hotel

Place: The restaurant and saloon of the Magnolia Hotel. The young man goes into the saloon at the end of the dinner that was served to him by a waitress.

Possible Characters: The young man. The waitress. The barkeeper. Two men at the bar. A card-playing woman who wears a gun. One or two other card players.

Possible Events: The young man asks the waitress if she would join him for a drink in the saloon. The two men at the bar talk about gold and philosophy to the barkeeper and to anyone else who will listen. The card players find that the woman card player is hiding an extra card somewhere.

Situation 3: At the Gold Mine

Place: The miners' log cabin. The miners are giving a goodbye party for the young man, who has decided to return to San Francisco to study mathematics.

Possible Characters: The young man. Partner 1, Partner 2, and Partner 3. Two people from the nearby settlement who are friends of the miners and who have brought cake and coffee to the party.

Possible Events: The miners and their friends try several ways to make the young man change his mind about leaving. He refuses, because the study of mathematics is very, very important to him.

Other Possible Events: Partner 3 enters sometime after the party has begun. He is carrying a large nugget of gold that he found just minutes ago. The gold weighs five pounds and is worth $750 a pound. How many people should share the money? How much money should each person get?

F. Discussion: Special Places, People, and Times

1. Have you ever seen a movie about the American West that included a scene with a gunfight in a saloon? If so, describe

it. If not, where do you think you could find such a movie? Would you be interested in watching it? Why, or why not?

2. What did you think of the young man in "How I Went to the Mines"? Did he do anything that you admired? that you thought was silly? that you thought was wrong? Is he someone you'd like to travel or work with? Why, or why not?

3. Many stories came to us from the lives of the people who moved west in the United States during the 1800s— pioneers, gold miners, cowboys, card players, gunfighters, lawmen, hunters, farmers—and from the lives of the Native Americans, or American Indians, who were already there. These stories, over many years, became an important part of American culture. Can you describe stories about special places, people, or times that in a similar way became important to the culture of another country?

G. Writing: A First-Person Narrative

When you wrote "A Speech to the Abolitionists" for "The Ingrate" (page 28), you wrote a *first-person narrative*—that is, a story (narrative) in which you used the first person ("I"). You wrote that narrative by answering questions about Joshua Leckler's life and experience. In this exercise, you will write a first-person narrative based on your own life and experience. Read the Guidelines for writing a narrative of 150–250 words.

Guidelines

In "How I Went to the Mines," a young man tries to do several things that his life has not prepared him to do. (He sleeps outside in the woods. He goes into a saloon. He experiences a gunfight.)

Write a narrative of 150–250 words. Tell about a time when you tried to do something that your life had not prepared you to do. Read the following questions before you write, and then write freely. You do not need to answer all the questions or to follow the order in which they are asked. They are here only to help guide your thoughts.

1. How old were you when this event (or these events) took place?
2. What was the thing you wanted or needed or were forced to do?

3. Until then, what did you know about this thing or situation or action?
4. How did you try to prepare yourself for the attempt?
5. What exactly did you do?
6. What surprises did you find during your attempt?
7. Who, if anyone, tried to help you?
8. Did you have good luck or bad luck in your attempt?
9. What was the result of your attempt?
10. How did you feel about the result?

4

PAUL'S CASE

❋

Adapted from the story by
WILLA CATHER

Willa Cather was born in Virginia in 1873. When she was ten, her
family moved to a farm in Nebraska. At that time, pioneer settlers
from the eastern United States were moving into the new state. Two of
Cather's famous novels, *My Antonia* and *O Pioneers!,* describe the
life of these early settlers. As a young woman, Cather taught English,
wrote for a newspaper, and edited a magazine in Pittsburgh,
Pennsylvania. Then she moved to New York to work at *McClure's*
magazine. Much of her later writing describes the painters, writers,
and theater people she met there. Although different from the farmers
of her youth, these artists were also pioneers—people who explored
unsettled areas of thought and feeling. And, like the early settlers,
they sometimes left society to begin a new exploration on their own.
Willa Cather died in 1947.

BEFORE YOU READ THE STORY

A. About the Author

Read the paragraph about Willa Cather on page 49. It tells us that Cather wrote about two very different kinds of people. What were they? What did they have in common?

B. The Pictures

1. Look at the picture on page 52. What do the faces of the men in the picture show? What does the face of the boy in the picture show? Where do you think this scene is taking place?
2. The picture on page 58 shows the same young man. In what ways does he look the same, and in what ways different, from the way he looks in the first picture? Where do you think he is, and what do you think he is doing?

C. Thinking About Conflict

"Paul's Case" shows us some well-known struggles or disagreements called **conflicts**: teenager against adult, student against teacher, son against father, artist against society, the lover of freedom against the world's rules. The story takes place in the first quarter of the twentieth century, but its themes are just as modern today. Of the conflicts mentioned above, can you think of one that has appeared in the news recently? Can you think of one that has been important in your own life?

D. Scanning for Context

Sometimes when we scan, we come across a particular word or phrase that seems to contain within it an important underlying idea or concept.

Scan Part I (pages 51–54) of "Paul's Case" until you find the words *usher*, *uniform*, and *aisle*. When you find each word, read further until you can write a definition of the word. Use words or phrases from the text or your own words. Try to complete the exercise in six minutes.

1. usher _____

2. uniform _____

3. aisle _____

At the beginning of Cather's story, Paul's teachers meet to discuss his **case**—that is, the special situation of a difficult student who does not behave as he should. Paul's **attitude**, the way he talks and presents himself, seems **contemptuous** to his teachers; they believe he finds them and their opinions unimportant. They are so **offended** by Paul that they make him leave school for a week, hoping that this **suspension** will change his behavior. But Paul cannot change. He is made sad by ordinary life and wants only the unnatural, **artificial** life of the theater. He wants to be **elegant,** like the rich, beautifully dressed people he sees there.

PAUL'S CASE

I

It was Paul's afternoon to appear before his teachers at Pittsburgh High School. He had been suspended a week ago. Now he was expected to explain his bad behavior. Paul entered the teachers' room, smooth and smiling. He had outgrown his clothes a little, and the velvet collar of his overcoat looked a little worn. But there was something elegant about him. He wore a jeweled pin in his neat tie. He had a red carnation in his coat. His teachers felt his appearance did not show the right attitude toward suspension.

2   Paul was tall for his age, and very thin. His large eyes had a glassy shine. He continually flashed them at people in an artificial way. His teachers found that offensive in a boy.

3   The principal asked him why he was there. Paul answered, politely enough, that he wanted to come back to school. This was a lie, but Paul was used to lying. He needed to lie to solve his problems. Then his teachers were asked to explain his behavior in class. They spoke with such anger that it was clear that Paul's case was no ordinary case. He was offensive in class. He had a contemptuous attitude toward his teachers. They attacked him like a pack of angry dogs.

4 Through all of this, Paul stood smiling, his lips open to show his teeth. Older boys than Paul had cried at such meetings. But Paul kept on flashing his eyes around him, always smiling. When he was told that he could go, he bowed gracefully, and went out. His bow, like the offensive red carnation, only showed his contempt.

5 The art teacher said what they all felt. "I don't really believe that smile is natural. There's something artificial about it. The boy is not strong, for one thing. There is something wrong about him."

6 His teachers left the meeting angry and unhappy. But Paul ran gracefully down the hall. He was whistling a song from the opera he was going to watch that night. He hoped some of the teachers would see how little he cared about the meeting.

7 Paul worked as an usher at Carnegie Hall. Since he was late that evening he decided to go straight to the concert. He was always excited while he got dressed in the usher's uniform. The uniform fit him better than the other boys, and he thought he looked elegant.

8 Paul was a model usher. Graceful and smiling, he ran up and down the aisles, showing people to their seats. He carried messages as though it was his greatest pleasure in life. As the theater filled, he became more and more excited. His cheeks and lips were red and his eyes flashed. It was as if the theater was a great party and Paul was the host. When the music began, Paul sat down in back. With a sigh he lost himself in the music. The first answering sigh of the violins seemed to free some wild excitement inside him. The lights danced before his eyes, and the concert hall flashed with color. Then the singer came on, and Paul forgot all about his teachers.

Paul liked

9 He always felt depressed after a concert. He hated to give up the excitement and color. Tonight he waited outside the hall for the singer. When she came out, he followed her across the street to the Schenley Hotel. The hotel stood large and lit up, for singers and actors and big businessmen. Paul had often hung around the hotel, watching the people go in and out. He wanted to enter that bright elegance and leave schoolteachers and problems behind him. He watched the singer pass through the shining glass doors. In that moment, Paul felt himself pass through with her. He imagined the

delicious platters of food that were brought to the dining room. He could almost see the green wine bottles in shining ice-buckets, like photographs in the newspapers.

10   A cold wind rose, and it began to rain hard. Paul was surprised to find himself standing outside. His boots were letting in water and his overcoat was wet. Rain fell between him and the lighted windows in front of him. He wondered if he would always have to stand outside in the cold, looking in. He turned and walked slowly to the bus stop.

"typo   The houses

II

11   Half an hour later, Paul got off the bus and walked down Cordelia Street to his house. All the houses looked alike. Clerks and small businessmen lived there, and raised large families. The children went to Sunday school, and were interested in geometry. They were just as alike each other as the houses were. Paul always felt hopeless and depressed when he walked down Cordelia Street. He had the feeling of sinking into ugliness, like water closing over his head. After the excitement of this evening he couldn't bear to see his room, with its ugly yellow wallpaper. Or the cold bathroom with the dirty tub, the broken mirror. Or his father, with his hairy legs sticking out from under his nightshirt. Paul was so late tonight that his father would be angry. Paul would have to explain, and to lie. He couldn't face it. He decided that he wouldn't go in.

12   He went around to the back of the house and found a basement window open. He climbed through and dropped down to the floor. He stood there, holding his breath, afraid of the noise he had made. But he heard nothing from upstairs. He carried a box over to the furnace to keep warm. He didn't try to sleep. He was horribly afraid of rats. And suppose his father had heard him, and came down and shot him as a thief? Then again, suppose his father came down with a gun, but Paul cried out in time to save himself? His father would be horrified to think he had nearly killed him. But what if his father wished Paul *hadn't* cried out, and *hadn't* saved himself? Paul entertained himself with these thoughts until daybreak.

13   On sunny Sunday afternoons, the people of Cordelia Street sat out on their front steps, the women in their Sunday clothes. Children played in the streets while their

parents talked. The women talked about sewing and children, the men gave advice about business and the cost of things. Paul sat there listening. The men were telling stories about the rich and powerful men who were their bosses. They owned palaces in Venice. They sailed yachts on the Mediterranean. They gambled at Monte Carlo. Paul's imagination was excited at the idea of becoming boss, but he had no mind for the clerk stage.

14   After supper was over, he helped dry the dishes. Then he asked nervously if he could go to George's for help with his geometry. His father asked him why he couldn't study with someone who lived nearer. And he shouldn't leave his homework until Sunday. But finally he gave him money for the bus. Paul ran upstairs to wash the smell of dishwater from his hands. He shook a few drops of cologne over his fingers. Then he left the house with his geometry book, very obvious, under his arm. The moment he left Cordelia Street and got on the bus, he shook off two days of deadening boredom. He began to live again.

15   Paul had a friend, Charley Edwards, who was a young actor. Paul spent every extra moment in Charley's dressing-room, helping him dress. It was at the theater and concert hall that Paul really lived. The rest was only a sleep and a forgetting. This was Paul's fairy tale, this was his secret love. The moment he breathed the smell behind the scenes, his imagination took fire. The moment the violins began to play, he shook off all stupid and ugly things.

16   In Paul's world, natural things were nearly always ugly. Perhaps that was why he thought artificiality was necessary to beauty. His life was full of Sunday-school picnics, saving money, good advice, and the smell of cooking. It was not that he wanted to become an actor or musician. What he wanted was to see theater, to breathe its air, to be carried away from it all.

17   After a night behind the scenes, Paul found school worse than ever. He hated the bare floors and empty walls. He hated the teachers: boring men who never wore carnations in their old suits. And he hated the women, with their dull dresses and high voices, who spoke so seriously about prepositions and adjectives. He couldn't bear to have the other students think he took these people seriously. He wanted them to see that school meant nothing to him. It was all a joke. He

showed his classmates pictures of his friends at the theater. He told them unbelievable stories of his midnight suppers with actors and musicians. He talked about the flowers he sent to his actor friends, and the trips they would take together.

18   Things went worse and worse at school. Paul was offensive to the teachers. He had no time for geometry, he was too busy helping his friends at the theater. Finally the principal went to Paul's father. Paul was taken out of school. He was put to work as a clerk for Denny & Carson. The manager of Carnegie Hall was told to get another usher. The doorman at the theater was told not to let him in. Charley Edwards promised not to see him again. The theater people were amused when they heard the stories Paul had told. They agreed that Paul was a bad case.

III

19   The train ran east through a January snowstorm. Paul woke up as the train whistled outside of New York City. He felt dirty and uncomfortable. He had taken the night train to avoid any Pittsburgh businessman who might have seen him at Denny & Carson.

20   When he arrived at the station he took a taxi to a large men's store. He spent two hours there, buying carefully: a suit, dress clothes, shirts and silk underwear. He drove on to a hat shop and a shoe shop. His last stop was at Tiffany's, where he chose silver brushes and a tie-pin. Then he had the taxi take him to the Waldorf Hotel. Paul went

21   When he was shown into his rooms on the eighth floor, he saw that everything was as it should be. Only one thing was missing. He ordered flowers brought up to his room. Outside the snow was falling wildly, but inside the air was soft and smelled of flowers. He was very tired. He had been in such a hurry, and had been under such pressure. He had come so far in the last twenty-four hours.

22   It had been wonderfully simple. When they shut him out of the theater and the concert hall, the whole thing was sure to happen. It was only a matter of when. The only thing that surprised Paul was his own courage. He had always been afraid. Even when he was a little boy he felt fear watching him from a dark corner. And Paul had done things that were not pretty to watch, he knew. But now he felt free of that—he had driven fear away.

23   Only yesterday he had been sent to the bank with Denny & Carson's money. There was more than $2,000 in checks, and nearly $1,000 in cash. He had slipped the thousand into his pocket, and left only the checks at the bank. He knew no one would notice for two or three days, and his father was away on business for the week. From the time he slipped the money into his pocket, and caught the train to New York, he had never lost his nerve.

24   When he woke up it was four o'clock. He dressed carefully and took a taxi up Fifth Avenue to Central Park. Snow fell against shop windows full of spring flowers. The park looked like a winter scene in the theater. Later, at dinner, he sat alone at a table near the window. The flowers, the white tablecloths, the many-colored wine glasses, the bright dresses of the women, the low music of the violins— all these things filled him with joy. Paul wondered why there were any honest men at all—this was what all the world was fighting for. He couldn't believe in Cordelia Street. He felt only contempt for those people. Had he ever lived there? Alone later, at the opera, he was not lonely. He had no wish to meet or know any of these elegant people. All he wanted was the right to be a part of the scene and watch.

25   The manager of the hotel was not suspicious. Paul drew no attention to himself. His pleasures were quiet ones. He loved to sit in the evenings in his living room. He enjoyed his flowers, his clothes, his cigarette, and his feeling of power. He could not remember a time when he had been so at peace with himself. He was glad not to have to lie, day after day. He had only lied to make people notice him. He wanted to prove his difference from the boys on Cordelia Street. Now he could be honest. He felt no guilt at what he had done. His golden days went by without a shadow. He made each one as perfect as he could.

26   On the eighth day after his arrival in New York, he saw the whole story in the Pittsburgh paper. The company of Denny & Carson reported that the boy's father had paid back what he stole. They would not send Paul to jail. His father thought he might be in New York. He was on his way East to find his son.

27   Paul felt terrible. The thought of returning to Cordelia Street, to Sunday school, to his ugly room, to old dishtowels, was worse than jail. He had the terrible feeling

that the music had stopped, the play was over. But later, at dinner, the violin and the flash of light and color had their old magic. He drank his wine wildly. He would show himself that he could finish the game with elegance. Was he not a very special person? Wasn't this the world where he belonged?

28   The next morning he woke up with a headache. He had never felt so depressed. Yet somehow he was not afraid. Perhaps he had looked into the dark corner where his terror had always waited. He saw everything clearly now. He had the feeling that he had made the best of it. He had lived the sort of life he was meant to live.

29   Paul took a taxi out into the country. Then he sent the taxi away and walked along the train tracks. The snow lay heavy on the ground. He climbed a little hill above the tracks, and sat down. He noticed that the carnations in his coat were dying in the cold. All the flowers he had seen that first night in New York must have gone the same way. They only had one bright breath of life. It was a losing game, it seemed, to fight against the world's advice. Paul took one of the carnations from his coat. He dug a hole in the snow, and carefully covered up the flower.

30   The sound of a train brought him back. He jumped to his feet, afraid that he might be too late. He was smiling nervously. His eyes moved left and right, as if someone was watching him. When the right moment came, he jumped. As he fell, he saw with regret all that he had left undone. The blue Mediterranean, the gold of Monte Carlo. He felt something hit his chest. His body was thrown through the air, on and on, further and faster. Then, his imagination flashed into black, and Paul dropped back into the immense design of things.

AFTER YOU READ THE STORY

A. Understanding the Plot

Answer the following questions with complete sentences.

1. Why does Paul have to come back to school one afternoon?
2. Why are his teachers angry with him?
3. Where does Paul go after the meeting? What is his job there?
4. What does Paul think about his neighborhood, Cordelia Street? What is his feeling about the world of the theater and concert hall?
5. Why is he taken out of school? What is he forced to do?
6. Where does Paul run away to? What does he do there?
7. How does he pay for the trip?
8. What happens to Paul after he reads the newspaper that tells what he has done?

B. Close Reading

Part I (pages 51–54)
The *italicized* words in the sentences below are keys to understanding the conflict between Paul and his teachers and between Paul's feelings about everyday life and the excitement of the theater. Answer the questions that follow the sentences. Paragraph numbers are given to help you find the correct answers.

1. Paul's *suspension* from school lasted one week. What had he done to deserve that punishment? (paragraph 3)
2. Paul's teachers were angry because he obviously was not interested in his lessons, and they saw this as a sign of *contempt*. When they asked if he wanted to come back to school, did he show contempt again? What did he answer? Why? (paragraph 3)
3. Paul's *attitude* toward life could be seen in the jeweled pin in his neat tie—a touch of *elegance*. What other such sign did he present to the world? (paragraph 1)
4. Paul's teachers didn't find his red carnation elegant or his flashing eyes attractive. On the contrary, they found these things *offensive*. As a result, what did they feel at the end of the meeting? (paragraph 6)

5. In the concert hall—a very *artificial* place—Paul worked as an usher, running up and down the aisles, showing people to their seats. How does this job make him feel? (paragraph 8)
6. Paul always felt *depressed* after a concert. Why? (paragraph 9)
7. Paul wanted to enter the bright *elegance* of the Schenley Hotel. Why? What does he imagine it is like inside? (paragraph 9)

Part II (pages 54–56)

In Part II, Cather continues to show us the contrast in Paul's mind between the real world of his neighborhood, Cordelia Street, and the dream world of the theater and concert hall. In this exercise, you are asked to recall the details that make up Cather's picture of Cordelia Street.

1. "In Paul's world, natural things were nearly always ugly." (paragraph 16) Reread paragraph 11, and then list eight things about Cordelia Street that Paul found ugly, boring, or depressing.
2. Where did Paul spend the night? How did he spend the night? Why did he spend it that way? (paragraphs 11, 12)
3. Paragraphs 11 and 13 introduced us to the people of Cordelia Street. Who were they? What kind of jobs did they hold? What did they talk about when they gathered on their front steps?
4. Before he left his house, how did Paul "get rid" of the feel of Cordelia Street? (paragraph 14)
5. When Paul was removed from school, what four things happened that removed him further from the world he loved and pushed him closer to the world he hated? (paragraph 18)

Part III (pages 56–59)

Flowers are important to Paul. In Part 1, he faces his teachers wearing a red carnation in his coat. In Part II, he tells his classmates that he sends flowers to his actor friends. In Part III, flowers remain important. Answer the following questions. Paragraph numbers are given to help you find the correct answers.

1. Why does Paul order flowers sent to his room? What do the flowers add to the room? (paragraph 21)

2. In the taxi, Paul notices two things about the shop windows, one outside, one inside. What are they? (paragraph 24)
3. At the train tracks, what does Paul understand about the flowers that he saw "that first night in New York"? Why does he bury one of his red carnations in the snow? (paragraph 29)

C. Vocabulary Practice

Complete the sentences below in a way that shows the meaning of the underlined word. The number of the paragraph where the word appears is in parentheses.

Example:

Paul enjoys being an <u>usher</u>. His job is <u>to show people to their</u>

<u>seats in the concert hall.</u> (paragraph 8)

1. Paul has <u>horrible</u> and even <u>horrifying</u> thoughts when he spends the night in the cellar. These thoughts are _____ _____ (paragraph 12)

2. Paul feels that natural things are ugly and boring. He is excited by the <u>artificial</u> world of the theater because _____ _____ (paragraph 16)

3. Paul steals $1,000 and runs away to New York City. He is surprised that he has the <u>courage</u> to do this, because _____ _____ (paragraph 22)

4. The hotel manager was not <u>suspicious</u> of Paul because _____ _____ (paragraph 25)

5. When Paul reads in the newspaper that his father is coming to New York City to look for him, he feels <u>terrible</u> because _____ (paragraph 27)

6. As he throws himself in front of the train, Paul feels <u>regret</u> for _____ _____ (paragraph 30)

D. Word Forms

Complete the sentences with the correct form of the words given.

1. (*offense / offend / offensive*)

   a. Paul's worst _____, in his teachers' eyes, was that he didn't take school seriously.

   b. They also found his elegant clothing _____ when worn at school.

   c. Paul was careful not to _____ his theater friends.

2. (*pressure / pressure / pressured*)

   a. His teachers tried to put _____ on Paul to change by suspending him for a week.

   b. Paul's father _____ him about doing his homework, but at last gave him money for the bus.

   c. By the time he arrived in New York City, Paul was feeling tired and _____ by all he had done in running away.

3. (*depression / depress / depressed*)

   a. Living on Cordelia Street didn't _____ Paul's neighbors as much as it did Paul.

   b. Paul fell into a _____ after he left the exciting world of the theater.

   c. Paul felt _____ but not afraid when he went out to throw himself under the train.

4. (*imagination / imagine / imaginative*)

   a. For a highly _____ boy like Paul, life on Cordelia Street seemed boring and unimportant.

   b. Paul's _____ was killed by school, but born again inside the theater.

   c. In New York City, Paul experienced for a short time the rich, elegant life he had always _____ living.

E. Language Activity: Interview, "Fairy Tales and Secret Loves"

Look again at what Cather tells us about the world of the theater and concert hall in Paul's mind (paragraph 15): "This was Paul's fairy tale, this was his secret love. The moment he breathed the smell behind the scenes, his imagination took fire. The moment the violins began to play, he shook off all stupid and ugly things."

In this exercise, you are asked to interview someone outside of your class. You want to find what it is that allows this person to "shake off all stupid and ugly things." Report the results of your interview to the whole class.

During the interview, you may want to ask some of the following questions:

- What do you do when you want to forget your problems?
- Is there a particular place you can go where your problems disappear, or where you feel you can be yourself?
- What activity makes you feel most happy, most relaxed, most yourself?
- What activity allows you to feel most free from other people's expectations of you?
- Do you feel most natural when you are completely alone, when you are alone in a crowd, or when you are with friends? Why do you think this is so?
- Do you ever, in your imagination, think about a career that you know you may not actually be able to have in real life? What is that career? Are you sure you won't try it?
- Do other people you know have secret dreams, secret loves? What is the strangest one you know of?

F. Discussion: "Paul's Case"

1. How did you feel about the ending of the story? Were you surprised? shocked? saddened? Did you feel that the ending had to happen the way it did? What other path might Paul have taken? Would that path have been within his character, as we came to know it in the story?
2. What is the meaning, in your opinion, of the final phrase: ". . . and Paul dropped back into the immense design of things." *Immense* means huge, unable to be measured. A *design* is a plan, or the working out of a plan: a project with

a purpose or aim. What do they mean when you put the two words together? Does this idea help us understand or accept Paul's death? Why, or why not?

3. The word *case* in the story's title tells us from the start that the "Paul" of the title will be an unusual young man. But how special is he? Do you think Paul's "case" is so unusual that it is unrealistic? Can you think of other "cases" that in some ways are similar to Paul's? Do you think modern society produces more or fewer cases like Paul's than the society of seventy-five to a hundred years ago? (What effect, for example, might TV and news stories about movie stars or famous athletes have on someone like Paul today?)

G. Writing: A Third-Person Narrative

In this writing exercise, you are asked to write a third-person narrative—that is, a narrative (story) using the third person (*he, she,* or *they*). Read the Guidelines for writing a four-paragraph narrative of 200–450 words.

Guidelines

In Part III of "Paul's Case," Willa Cather shows us many details of Paul's life as he realizes his deepest wish: to live a life of complete freedom in elegant surroundings. The details of Paul's brief feeling of complete joy are memorable: his new clothes, the silver brushes, the elegant rooms at the Waldorf Hotel, the flowers, a night at the opera. In fact, Paul realizes his dream completely, if very briefly.

Your composition should describe another case of a person trying to make real a dream or realize a deep wish. Use your own experience, the experience of the person you interviewed in exercise E on page 64, the experience of someone you know, or an experience out of your imagination. In any case, you are asked to write in the third person, using *he* or *she* to talk about your main character.

Paragraph 1: The Theme

Begin with a brief statement of your theme. Consider these questions: What is the deep wish or great dream that you are writing about? Who is the person whose imagination is "on fire" with this wish or dream?

Paragraph 2: Introduction

Introduce fully the dream or wish itself. Where, when, how, and why did the person start feeling this strong wish? What did the person want to do? How did he or she think it might be possible to do it?

Paragraph 3: The Main Body of the Composition

Write about what the person did in trying to reach the dream and what happened, step by step. Did the person realize the dream or not? What did other people do to help with the success or cause the failure of the attempt? How much of the success or failure was caused by the person's character?

Paragraph 4: The Conclusion

Write about how the person felt about the success or failure of his or her attempt to make real a dream, to realize a deep wish. What did the success or failure mean to the person? How, if at all, did it change the person? What did the person learn from the attempt he or she made?

5

A JURY OF HER PEERS

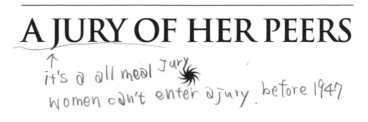

it's a all meal Jury
women can't enter ajury, before 1947

Adapted from the story by
SUSAN GLASPELL

Susan Glaspell was born in 1882, in Davenport, Iowa. She worked for a newspaper there until she earned enough to support herself by writing fiction. She wrote a lot—ten novels and more than forty stories. But she is also well known for her plays. She and her husband founded a famous theater, the Provincetown Playhouse, in Provincetown, Massachusetts (on Cape Cod), in 1915. Her husband directed plays by young, unknown writers. Many of these writers later became famous. Glaspell first wrote "A Jury of Her Peers" as a play called *Trifles*—the word means "small things of little value." Later, she rewrote the play as a story. Glaspell often wrote about people trapped by the choices they make in life. She died in 1948.

BEFORE YOU READ THE STORY

A. About the Author

Read the paragraph about Susan Glaspell on page 67. What is the difference between *Trifles* and "A Jury of Her Peers"?

B. The Picture

Look at the picture on page 75. One woman is holding a **quilt block** in her hand. A **quilt** is a kind of bed cover. Small pieces (blocks) of cloth are sewed together to make a large cover. Then the quilt cover is sewed to heavier material to make the cover warm. There are two ways to fasten the top cover to the heavier material. One is to knot it—to tie it on with small knots. The other is to quilt it—to sew it on with small stitches.

C. Thinking About a Jury of Your Peers

A **jury** is a group of people who study the facts in a law case and give a decision based on those facts. A **peer** is an equal, someone of the same value or quality or ability. In English and American law, each person accused of a crime has the right to argue his or her case before "a jury of his or her peers." If you could choose a jury of your peers to judge an action you had taken, which people would you choose? Why?

D. Skimming to Get an Impression

Quickly skim Part I (pages 69–70) of "A Jury of Her Peers," for no more than sixty to ninety seconds. Then try to answer the following questions.

1. Does the story take place in a warm climate or a cold one?
2. Does the story take place in a city or in the country?
3. Are the characters in the story men or women, or both?
4. Does the story seem funny or serious to you?

In this famous story by Susan Glaspell, a crime has taken place: A man lies dead with a **rope** around his neck. The local policeman, called a **sheriff,** must find who killed him. To do this, he must find signs, or **clues,** that tell him what happened. He must discover what reason, or **motive,** the killer might have had. Then the government lawyer, or **attorney,** can bring the case to a court of law.

A JURY OF HER PEERS

I

Martha Hale opened the storm door and felt the cutting north wind. She ran back inside for her big <u>wool</u> shawl. She was unhappy with what she saw there in her kitchen. Her bread was all ready for mixing, half the flour sifted and half unsifted. She hated to see things half done. But it was no ordinary thing that called her away. It was probably further from ordinary than anything that had ever happened in Dickson County.

2   She had been sifting flour when the sheriff drove up with his horse and buggy to get Mr. Hale. Sheriff Peters had asked Mrs. Hale to come, too. His wife was nervous, he said with a grin. She wanted another woman to come along. So Martha Hale had dropped everything right where it was.

3   "Martha!" her husband's voice came, "don't keep the folks waiting out here in the cold!"

4   She tied the wool shawl tighter and climbed into the buggy. Three men and a woman were waiting for her. Martha Hale had met Mrs. Peters, the sheriff's wife, at the county fair. Mrs. Peters didn't seem like a sheriff's wife. She was small and thin and ordinary. She didn't have a strong voice. But Mr. Peters certainly did look like a sheriff. He was a heavy man with a big voice, very friendly to folks who

followed the law. But now, Mrs. Hale thought, he was going to the Wrights' house as a sheriff, not a friend.

5   The Wrights' house looked lonely this cold March morning. It had always been a lonely-looking house. It was down in a valley, and the poplar trees around it were lonely-looking trees. The men were talking about what had happened there: her husband, Sheriff Peters, and the county attorney, Mr. Henderson. She looked over at Mrs. Peters.

6   "I'm glad you came with me," Mrs. Peters said nervously.

7   When the buggy reached the doorstep, Martha Hale felt she could not go inside. She had often said to herself, "I must go over and see Minnie Foster." She still thought of her as Minnie Foster, though for twenty years she had been Mrs. Wright. But there was always something to do, and Minnie Foster would go from her mind. She felt sad that she had come only *now*.

8   The men went over to stand by the stove. The women stood together by the door. At first, they didn't even look around the kitchen.

9   "Now, Mr. Hale," the sheriff began. "Before we move things around, you tell Mr. Henderson what you saw when you came here yesterday morning."

II

10   Mrs. Hale felt nervous for her husband. Lewis Hale often lost his way in a story. She hoped he would tell it straight this time. Unnecessary things would just make it harder for Minnie Foster.

11   "Yes, Mr. Hale?" the county attorney said.

12   "I started to town with a load of potatoes," Mrs. Hale's husband began. "I came along this road, and I saw the house. I said to myself, 'I'm going to see John Wright about the telephone.' They will bring a telephone out here if I can get somebody else to help pay for it. I'd spoken to Wright before, but he said folks talked too much already. All *he* asked for was peace and quiet. I guess you know how much he talked himself. But I thought I would ask him in front of his wife. All the women like the telephone. In this lonely road it would be a good thing. Not that he cared much about what his wife wanted . . ."

13   Now there he was!—saying things he didn't need to say. Mrs. Hale tried to catch her husband's eye, but luckily the attorney interrupted him with:

14   "Just tell what happened when you got there, Mr. Hale."

15   Mr. Hale began again, more carefully. "I knocked at the door. But it was all quiet inside. I knew they must be up—it was past eight o'clock. I knocked again, louder, and I thought I heard someone say, 'Come in.' I opened the door—this door"—Mr. Hale pointed toward the door where the two women stood. "And there, in that rockingchair"— he pointed to it— "sat Mrs. Wright."

16   "How did she—look?" the county attorney asked.

17   "Well," said Hale, "she looked—strange."

18   "How do you mean—strange?"

19   The attorney took out a notebook and pencil. Mrs. Hale did not like that pencil. She kept her eye on her husband, as if to tell him, "No unnecessary things. They'll just go into that notebook and make trouble." Hale spoke carefully, as if the pencil made him think more slowly.

20   "Well, she didn't seem to know what she was going to do next. I said, 'How do, Mrs. Wright. It's cold isn't it?' And she said, 'Is it?,' and sat there fingering her apron, nervous-like.

21   "Well, I was surprised. She didn't ask me to come in and sit down, but just sat there, not even looking at me. And so I said, 'I want to see John.'

22   "And then she—laughed. I guess you'd call it a laugh.

23   "I said, a little sharp, 'Can I see John?'

24   " 'No,' she said, kind of dull. 'Isn't he home?' said I. 'Yes,' says she, 'he's home.' 'Then why can't I see him?' I asked her. Now I was angry. 'Because he's dead,' says she— all quiet and dull. She fingered her apron some more.

25   " 'Why, where is he?' I said, not knowing *what* to say.

26   "She just pointed upstairs—like this," said Hale, pointing. "Then I said, 'Why, what did he die of?'

27   " 'He died of a rope around his neck,' says she, and just went on fingering her apron."

28   Nobody spoke. Everyone looked at the rockingchair as if they saw the woman who had sat there yesterday.

29   "And what did you do then?" The attorney at last interrupted the silence.

30   "I went upstairs." Hale's voice fell. "There he was— lying on the—he was dead, all right. I thought I'd better not touch anything. So I went downstairs.

31   " 'Who did this, Mrs. Wright?' I said, sharp, and she stops fingering her apron. 'I don't know,' she says. 'You don't know?' said I. 'Weren't you sleeping in the same bed with him? Somebody tied a rope around his neck and killed him, and you didn't wake up?'

32   " 'I didn't wake up,' she says after me.

33   "I may have looked as if I didn't see how that could be. After a minute she said, 'I sleep sound.'

34   "I thought maybe she ought to tell her story first to the sheriff. So I went as fast as I could to the nearest telephone—over at the Rivers' place on High Road. Then I came back here to wait for Sheriff Peters.

35   "I thought I should talk to her. So I said I had stopped by to see if John wanted to put in a telephone. At that, she started to laugh, and then she stopped and looked frightened. . . ."

36   The attorney spoke to the sheriff. "I guess we'll go upstairs first—then out to the barn and around there. You made sure yesterday that there's nothing important here in the kitchen?"

37   "Nothing here but kitchen things," said the sheriff with a laugh.

38   The attorney was searching in the cupboard. After a minute he pulled out his hand, all sticky.

39   "Here's a nice mess," he said angrily.

40   "Oh—her fruit," Mrs. Peters said. She looked at Mrs. Hale. "She was worried about her fruit when it turned cold last night. She said the stove might go out, and the jars might break."

41   Mrs. Peters' husband began to laugh. "Well, how about that for a woman! Held in jail for murder, and worrying about her jars of fruit!"

42   The attorney answered, "I guess before we finish with her, she may have something more important to worry about."

43   "Oh, well," Mr. Hale said, "women are used to worrying about nothing."

44   "And yet," said the attorney, "what would we do without the ladies?" He smiled at the women, but they did not speak, did not smile back.

45   The lawyer washed his hands and dried them on the dishtowel.

46   "Dirty towels!" he said. "Not much of a housekeeper, eh, ladies?" He kicked some messy pans under the sink.

47   "There's a lot of work to do around a farm," Mrs. Hale said sharply. "And men's hands aren't always as clean as they might be."

48   "Ah! You feel a duty to your sex, I see!" He laughed. "But you and Mrs. Wright were neighbors. I guess you were friends, too."

49   "I've not seen much of her these years."

50   "And why was that? You didn't like her?"

51   "I liked her well enough. Farmers' wives have their hands full, Mr. Henderson. And then—it never seemed like a very happy place . . ."

52   "You mean the Wrights didn't get on very well together?"

53   "No. I don't mean anything. But I don't think a place would be happier if John Wright was in it."

54   "I'd like to talk to you more about that, Mrs. Hale. But first we'll look upstairs."

55   The sheriff said to the attorney, "I suppose anything Mrs. Peters does will be all right? She came to take Mrs. Wright some clothes—and a few little things."

56   "Of course," said the attorney. "Mrs. Peters is one of us. Maybe you women may come on a clue to the motive—and that's the thing we need."

57   Mr. Hale smiled, ready to make a joke. "Yes, but would the women know a clue if they did come upon it?"

III

58   The women stood silent while the men went upstairs. Then Mrs. Hale began to clean the messy pans under the sink.

59   "I would hate to have men coming into my kitchen, looking around and talking about my housework."

60   "Of course, it's their duty," Mrs. Peters said. But Mrs. Hale was looking around the kitchen herself. She saw a box of sugar. Next to it was a paper bag—half full.

61   "She was putting this in there," she said to herself. Work begun and not finished? She saw the table—a dishtowel lay on it. One half of the table was clean. What had interrupted Minnie Foster?

62 "I must get her things from the cupboard," Mrs. Peters said.

63 Together they found the few clothes Mrs. Wright had asked for. Mrs. Hale picked up an old black skirt.

64 "My, John Wright hated to spend money!" she said. "She used to wear pretty clothes and sing in the church, when she was Minnie Foster . . ." Martha Hale looked at Mrs. Peters and thought: she doesn't care that Minnie Foster had pretty clothes when she was a girl. But then she looked at Mrs. Peters again, and she wasn't sure. In fact, she had never been sure of Mrs. Peters. She seemed so nervous, but her eyes looked as if they could see a long way into things.

65 "Is this all you want to take to the jail?" Martha Hale asked.

66 "No, she wanted an apron and her woolen shawl." Mrs. Peters took them from the cupboard.

67 "Mrs. Peters!" cried Mrs. Hale suddenly. "Do you think she did it?"

68 Mrs. Peters looked frightened. "Oh, I don't know," she said.

69 "Well, I don't think she did," Mrs. Hale said. "Asking for her apron and her shawl. Worrying about her fruit."

70 "Mr. Peters says it looks bad for her," Mrs. Peters answered. "Saying she didn't wake up when someone tied that rope around his neck. Mr. Henderson said that what this case needs is a motive. Something to show anger—or sudden feeling."

71 "Well, I think it's kind of low to lock her up in jail, and then come out here to look for clues in her own house," said Martha Hale.

72 "But, Mrs. Hale," said the sheriff's wife, "the law is the law."

73 Mrs. Hale turned to re-light the stove. "How would you like to cook on this broken thing year after year—?"

74 Mrs. Peters looked from the broken stove to the bucket of water on the sink. Water had to be carried in from outside. "I know. A person gets so *down*—and loses heart."

75 And again Mrs. Peters' eyes had that look of seeing into things, of seeing through things.

76 "Oh, look, Mrs. Hale. She was sewing a quilt." Mrs. Peters picked up a sewing basket full of quilt blocks.

77   The women were studying the quilt as the men came downstairs. Just as the door opened, Mrs. Hale was saying, "Do you think she was going to quilt it, or just knot it?"

78   "Quilt it or knot it!" laughed the sheriff. "They're worrying about a quilt!" The men went out to look in the barn.

79   Then Mrs. Peters said in a strange voice, "Why, look at this one." She held up a quilt block. "The sewing. All the rest were sewed so nice. But this one is so *messy*—"

80   Mrs. Hale took the quilt block. She pulled out the sewing and started to replace bad sewing with good.

81   "Oh, I don't think we ought to touch anything . . ." Mrs. Peters said helplessly.

82   "I'll just finish this end," said Mrs. Hale, quietly.

83   "Mrs. Hale?"

84   "Yes, Mrs. Peters?"

85   "What do you think she was so *nervous* about?"

86   "Oh, *I* don't know. I don't know that she was— nervous. Sometimes I sew badly when I'm tired."

87   She looked quickly at Mrs. Peters, but Mrs. Peters was looking far away. Later she said in an ordinary voice, "Here's a bird cage. Did she have a bird, Mrs. Hale? It seems kind of funny to think of a bird here. I wonder what happened to it."

88   "Oh, probably the cat got it."

89   "But look, the door has been broken. It looks as if someone was rough with it."

90   Their eyes met, worrying and wondering.

91   "I'm glad you came with me, Mrs. Hale. It would be lonely for me—sitting here alone."

92   "I *wish* I had come over here sometimes when she was here," answered Mrs. Hale. "I stayed away because it wasn't a happy place. Did you know John Wright, Mrs. Peters?"

93   "Not really. They say he was a good man."

94   "Well—good," Mrs. Hale said. "He didn't drink, and paid his bills. But he was a hard man. His voice was like the north wind that cuts to the bone. You didn't know—her, did you, Mrs. Peters?"

95   "Not until they brought her to the jail yesterday."

96   "She was—she was like a little bird herself. . . . Why don't you take the quilt blocks in to her? It might take up her mind."

97 "That's a nice idea, Mrs. Hale," agreed the sheriff's wife. She took more quilt blocks and a small box out of the sewing basket.

98 "What a pretty box," Mrs. Hale said. "That must be something she had from a long time ago, when she was a girl." Mrs. Hale opened the box. Quickly her hand went to her nose.

99 Mrs. Peters bent closer. "It's the bird," she said softly. "Someone broke its neck."

100 Just then the men came in the door. Mrs. Hale slipped the box under the quilt blocks.

101 "Well, ladies," said the county attorney, "have you decided if she was going to quilt it or knot it?" He smiled at them.

102 "We think," began the sheriff's wife nervously, "that she was going to—knot it."

103 "That's interesting, I'm sure," he said, not listening. "Well, there's no sign that someone came in from the outside. And it was their own rope. Now let's go upstairs again . . ." The men left the kitchen again.

104 "She was going to bury the bird in that pretty box," said Mrs. Hale.

105 "When I was a girl," said Mrs. Peters softly, "my kitten— there was a boy who murdered it, in front of my eyes. If they hadn't held me back, I would have—hurt him."

106 They sat without speaking or moving.

107 "Wright wouldn't like the bird. A thing that sang. *She* used to sing. He killed that, too," Mrs. Hale said slowly.

108 "Of course, we don't *know* who killed the bird," said Mrs. Peters.

109 "I knew John Wright," Mrs. Hale answered. "There had been years and years of—nothing. Then she had a bird to sing to her. It would be so—silent—when it stopped."

110 "I know what silence is," Mrs. Peters said in a strange voice. "When my first baby died, after two years . . ."

111 "Oh, I *wish* I'd come over here sometimes. *That* was a crime!" Mrs. Hale cried.

112 But the men were coming back. "No, Peters, it's all clear. Except the reason for doing it. If there was some real *clue* . . . Something to show the jury . . . You go back to town, sheriff. I'll stay and look around some more."

113   Mrs. Hale looked at Mrs. Peters. Mrs. Peters was looking at her.

114   "Do you want to see what Mrs. Peters is bringing to the jail?" the sheriff asked the attorney.

115   "Oh, I guess the ladies haven't picked up anything very dangerous," he answered. "After all, a sheriff's wife is married to the law. Did you ever think of your duty that way, Mrs. Peters?"

116   "Not—just that way," said Mrs. Peters quietly.

117   The men went out to get the buggy, and the women were alone for one last moment.

118   Mrs. Hale pointed to the sewing basket. In it was the thing that would keep another woman in jail.

119   For a moment Mrs. Peters did not move. Then she ran to get the box. She tried to put it in her little handbag, but it didn't fit.

120   There was the sound of the door opening. Martha Hale took the box and put it quickly in her big pocket.

121   "Well, Peters," said the county attorney jokingly, "at least we found out that she was not going to quilt it. She was going to—what do you call it, ladies?"

122   Mrs. Hale put her hand against her pocket. "We call it—knot it, Mr. Henderson."

AFTER YOU READ THE STORY

A. Understanding the Plot

Answer the following questions with complete sentences.

1. What was Martha Hale doing when the sheriff arrived? Why did the sheriff want her to come with the others?
2. What did Lewis Hale find when he stopped at the Wright's house?
3. What do the men say about Mrs. Wright's housekeeping?
4. What do the sheriff and the attorney need to find for the jury?
5. What do the women notice about one of the quilt blocks? What does Martha Hale do with it?

6. What was in the small box the women found in the sewing basket?
7. What does Martha Hale do with the box? Why?

B. Close Reading

Part I (pages 69–70)

In Part I we are introduced to many people. To understand "who's who," we have to read closely. For each description below, write the letter identifying the person who fits the description. Some names are used more than once.

a. Mrs. Hale   d. Minnie Foster   f. Mr. Henderson
b. Mrs. Peters   e. Mr. Peters   g. Mr. and Mrs. Wright
c. Mr. Hale

_f_ 1. He is the county attorney.

_e_ 2. He saw something very unusual at the Wrights' house yesterday morning.

_b_ 3. She is small and thin and has a weak voice.

_a_ 4. She was making bread when the others came to her house.

_d_ 5. She became Mrs. Wright.

_g_ 6. All the others were going to their house.

_e_ 7. He is the county sheriff, and a big man.

_c_ 8. He asked his wife not to keep everybody waiting in the buggy, out in the cold.

_b_ 9. She was glad that Martha had come on this trip.

_a_ 10. She hated to leave things half done, but this situation was very unusual.

Part II (pages 70–73)

Often, a writer will use dialog that suggests, rather than states directly, how a character feels. This kind of suggestion is called *implication*, or *implied meaning*. The following sentences from Part II are examples of implied meaning. The questions that follow ask you to tell what the words of each speaker *imply*. Paragraph numbers are given to help you find the dialog in the story.

1. *"Nothing here but kitchen things," said the sheriff with a laugh.* (paragraph 37)

    What is implied here by the sheriff's laugh? What does he think about the value of "kitchen things"?

2. *"Well, how about that for a woman! Held in jail for murder, and worrying about her jars of fruit!"* (paragraph 41)

    What does the sheriff imply about the woman's interest in her jars of fruit? What does he imply about women generally?

3. *"Oh, well," Mr. Hale said, "women are used to worrying about nothing."* (paragraph 43)

    What does Mr. Hale imply about the seriousness of women's concerns generally?

4. *"And yet," said the attorney, "what would we do without the ladies?"* (paragraph 44)

    The attorney seems to be saying that "the ladies" are valuable to "us." But he implies something different. What is it? Read the rest of paragraph 44. What do Mrs. Hale and Mrs. Peters imply by the way they react to the attorney's words?

5. *"There's a lot of work to do around a farm," Mrs. Hale said sharply. "And men's hands aren't always as clean as they might be."* (paragraph 47)

    What does Mrs. Hale imply here about the habits of men on a farm?

Part III (pages 73–78)

1. What are the clues that lead Mrs. Hale and Mrs. Peters to an understanding of what Mrs. Wright did, and why she did it?

2. With a partner, reread Part III and find the specific clues that the two women discovered. There are at least four important ones, as well as some smaller ones. Be prepared to describe the clues and tell why they are important.

C. Vocabulary Practice

Match the words in the left column with the correct definition in the right column. Then write your own sentence that shows the meaning of each word.

1. __c__ county   **a.** what causes a person to do something
2. __e__ attorney   **b.** an unlawful killing
3. __d__ clue   **c.** a division of a state, with certain legal and governing powers
4. __b__ murder   **d.** something that points to the solution of a problem
5. __a__ motive   **e.** an officer of a court of law

6. (*county*) _____

_____

7. (*attorney*) _____

_____

8. (*clue*) _____

_____

9. (*murder*) _____

_____

10. (*motive*) _____

_____

D. Word Forms

The chart below shows the noun, adjective, and adverb forms of four words.

Noun	Adjective	Adverb
duty	dutiful	dutifully
mess	messy	messily
nervousness	nervous	nervously
peace	peaceful	peacefully

For each group of sentences below, choose one group of word forms from the chart and place the correct forms of the word in the blank spaces.

1. a. Although Mr. Wright liked a quiet life, he was not a

   _____ man.

   b. After the sheriff arrested her, Mrs. Wright went

   _____ to jail.

   c. Mrs. Hale's _____ of mind was broken by news

   of Wright's murder.

2. a. Mrs. Hale felt _____ about her husband's way

   of telling a story.

   b. Mrs. Wright tried to hide her _____ by laughing.

   c. Mrs. Peters looked away _____ from Mrs. Hale.

3. a. When the attorney said that Mrs. Peters was "one of us,"

   he wanted to remind her that she had a _____ to

   follow the law.

   b. Is Mrs. Hale a less _____ woman than Mrs. Peters?

   c. Every summer Mrs. Wright _____ made jars of

   fruit for winter use.

4. a. Mrs. Wright tells the attorney that there are good reasons

   for _____ housekeeping.

   b. The broken fruit jars made a _____ in the

   cupboard.

   c. Mrs. Wright's pots and pans were pushed _____

   under the sink.

E. Language Activity: A Trial

The class will act out the trial of Mrs. Wright, who has been arrested for murdering her husband.

Choose a role:

- The *defendant*—the person accused of the crime (that is, Mrs. Wright); she will agree to be questioned at her trial.
- The *judge*—the person who manages or oversees the trial.
- The *jury*—the people (twelve of them on actual juries in the United States) who will decide whether the defendant is guilty or innocent.
- The *prosecuting attorney*—the lawyer who must prove to the jury that Mrs. Wright is guilty, that she murdered her husband.
- The *defense attorney*—the person who must defend Mrs. Wright.
- The *witnesses*—people who answer questions asked by the attorneys; they tell what they know and describe what they saw. They promise to tell "the truth, the whole truth, and nothing but the truth." The witnesses in this case are Sheriff and Mrs. Peters, Mr. and Mrs. Hale, and the county attorney. Remember: Mrs. Peters and Mrs. Hale believe that Mrs. Wright did kill her husband. But they do not want her to go to prison for life because of that.

Now, begin the trial:

1. The *judge* will organize and direct the trial, give instructions to the jury, and may interrupt the lawyer or witnesses at any time.
2. The *prosecuting attorney* will ask the defendant and each witness three to five questions.
3. The *defense attorney* will then ask questions of the defendant and the witnesses.
4. The attorneys will give brief final arguments to the *jury*, trying to convince the jurors of the guilt or innocence of the defendant.
5. The jury will discuss the case in the time allowed by the judge, and then report its decision to the judge.
6. If the jury decides that Mrs. Wright is guilty, the *judge* must decide her punishment.

F. Discussion: Duty and Behavior

1. An important theme that Glaspell explores in "A Jury of Her Peers" is the behavior, activities, and duties of men and women many years ago in a small country town. Using examples of behavior from the story, discuss what men seemed to expect from women at that time and in that place, and what women seemed to expect from men. (Look back at paragraphs 2, 3, 46, 55, 56, 115, and 116.) Do you think men and women behave in similar ways today? If so, at what times? in what places?

2. What do Mrs. Hale and Mrs. Peters do with the clues that they find? Do these clues prove that Mrs. Wright murdered her husband? Is it wrong of them not to give the clues to the sheriff? Why, or why not? Mrs. Hale and Mrs. Peters are Mrs. Wright's peers. In what sense do they also become her jury?

G. Writing: A Dialog

"A Jury of Her Peers" is told almost completely in dialog—there is very little description. Write a page of dialog: a conversation among Mrs. Hale, Mrs. Peters, and Mrs. Wright. Mrs. Hale and Mrs. Peters visit Mrs. Wright in the county jail. They bring her the things she has asked for. What do they talk about?

Example:

Mrs. Hale: Good morning, Mrs. Wright. We've brought you some things from your house.

Mrs. Wright: Thank you. You're very kind.

Mrs. Peters: We brought the clothes you asked for, Mrs. Wright. And your sewing basket. With your quilt blocks.

Mrs. Hale: Yes. But there was . . . well, there was another thing in the sewing basket that we didn't bring.

Mrs. Wright: Another thing? I . . . I can't remember well. What was it?

6

THE WHALE HUNT

❋

Adapted from the novel *Moby Dick* by
HERMAN MELVILLE

Herman Melville was born in 1819 in New York City. Although his parents were wealthy, his father lost his business and died when Melville was twelve. After he finished school, Melville worked for a short time in his brother's store and later in a bank; but neither job interested him. When he was nineteen, he went to sea on a trading ship to England. Three years later, in 1841, he went to sea again, this time on a whaling ship, the *Acushnet*. Melville spent four years on the whaling ship in the Pacific Ocean. His many adventures at sea formed the subject of several popular novels he wrote after returning from his voyages. The following story, "The Whale Hunt," is taken from his most famous novel, *Moby Dick*, published in 1851. The novel tells the adventures of a whaling ship, the *Pequod*, as it hunts Moby Dick, a huge white sperm whale. *Moby Dick* is considered one of the greatest of all American novels, but it was not very popular when it was first published. During the last twenty-five years of his life, Melville worked as a customs inspector in New York City. He wrote poetry during these years, but his early popularity fell away. Just before his death in 1891, he completed another book about life at sea, *Billy Budd*, which brought him to public attention once more.

BEFORE YOU READ THE STORY

A. About the Author

Read the paragraph about Melville on page 85. What experiences in his life did he use in his most famous writings? What was the *Pequod*, and what was Moby Dick?

B. The Pictures

1. Look at the picture on page 88. What do we see in the front of the picture? What is happening farther out on the water?
2. What is happening to the boat on page 94? Why do you think there were six men in the boat?

C. Thinking About the Old Whaling Days

Until late in the nineteenth century, men and women sailed the seas in wind-powered wooden ships. Fishermen and whale hunters used hand tools and simple steel or iron weapons. Imagine what it would be like on a wooden sailboat in a huge storm or during a period of no wind. What would it be like to spend months or even years away from land and family? What would it be like to hunt a huge animal like a whale with just a few men in a small boat? In the past 100 years, what are some of the changes in fishing or whale hunting that you know about? What dangers have not changed?

D. Scanning for Numbers

Sometimes, to find dates or numbers in a piece of writing, we need to do not only fast reading but a little addition or subtraction. Scan the paragraph on Melville on page 85 and do the simple math to find the dates or numbers asked for in the following questions.

1. In what year did Melville's father die?
2. In what year did Melville first go to sea?
3. How old was Melville when he went whaling on the *Acushnet*?
4. In what year did Melville begin work as a customs inspector in New York City?
5. How old was Melville when he died?

KEY WORDS

This story describes how the sailors, or **crew,** on a whaling ship hunted the **sperm whale** many, many years ago. The oil from those huge ocean animals was used in oil lamps before the invention of electricity. The front of a ship is called the **bow** and the back, the **stern.** The direction toward which the wind blows is called **leeward.** Sperm whales swim in groups, or **schools.** They come to the surface to breathe, and in breathing they "blow" a jet of water out of the tops of their heads that can be seen from far away. In the old days, small boats were lowered with crewmen from the large whaling ship to chase the whales and kill them by throwing **harpoons**—long wooden weapons with sharp metal points.

yard=meter

bow
stern
leeward
harpoon

endangered /
extinct } animal

THE WHALE HUNT

please find 3 new (words) vocabuly!

I

It was a hot, still afternoon. Storm clouds were gathering overhead. The whaling ship, *Pequod,* out of Nantucket, sailed smoothly across the lead-gray sea. The seamen were lazily lying on deck, or staring from the masts out to sea. All the men were still—still, too, the gray waters. Each silent sailor turned to his own dreaming.

2   I, Ishmael, was one of that crew. I had signed onto the *Pequod* in Nantucket with Queequeg, a Polynesian harpooner of great strength and skill. We had become friends sailing with these men for many empty days, with no sight of a whale. We had worked with the men; we had eaten, sung, and shouted with them. Now Queequeg and I sat with the others on deck, our hands slowly working with ropes and tools, our minds lost in thought and silence.

3   Suddenly I awoke to a cry so strange, so wild, that the rope fell from my hand. I stood looking up at the dark clouds from which that voice had dropped like a wing. High up in the highest mast was our lookout, Tashtego, an Indian from Martha's Vineyard Island in Massachusetts. His

body was reaching eagerly forward, his hand pointing straight ahead. His wild cry was the cry of whalemen all over the seas, from lookouts high up in the masts. But Tashtego's was the most unearthly and musical voice of all.

4   "There she blows! There! There! There! She blows! She blows!"

5   "Where-away?"

6   "There, to leeward, about two miles off! A school of them! Sperm whales, men!"

7   Instantly, everything was moving as we prepared for the hunt.

8   The sperm whale blows its jets of air and water as regularly as a clock ticks. This is how whalemen know them from other kinds of whale. The sperm whale is a clever, even tricky animal when it knows it is being hunted. But these whales had not seen us yet. Therefore the *Pequod* was now kept away from the wind, and she went gently rolling before it. We expected the whales to rise up in front of our bow.

9   The men not already on deck dropped down from the masts on ropes. The tubs that held ropes for the harpoons were set out on deck. The boat crews gathered by their boats. We swung the four boats from the deck of the *Pequod* out over the sea.

10   "All ready, Fedallah?" Captain Ahab cried to his harpooner, a dark, dangerous-looking man from the East Asian islands.

11   "Ready," was the half-hissed reply. Fedallah wore a black Chinese jacket; his white hair was wrapped round and round his head. He had the hard, silent, deadly look that ordinary people see only in fearful dreams.

12   "Lower the boats, then, do you hear? Lower away!" Captain Ahab shouted to the boat crew chiefs. The four boats were quickly lowered. The eager crews acted with an unconscious daring that is unknown in other professions. They jumped goat-like from the high deck of the *Pequod* down into the boats rolling on the waves below.

13   Captain Ahab stood tall in the stern of his boat. "Spread yourselves widely, all boats," he called to Starbuck, Stubb and Flask, the other boat crew chiefs. "You, Flask, pull out more to leeward."

14   "Aye, aye, Sir," little Flask answered happily. He swung around the great oar that steered his boat. "Lay back on

those oars!" he ordered his crew. "There! There again! There she blows right ahead, boys! Lay back!"

15   Starbuck was chief of my boat. Like the other crew chiefs, he stood in the stern of the boat holding the steering oar. We faced him, our backs to the whales ahead. As we headed past Stubb's boat, we could hear him talking to his crew: "Pull, pull on those oars, my fine hearts! Pull, my children, pull, my little ones," he called in a voice that was strong and low, smooth and musical. "Why don't you break your backbones, my boys? Still asleep, are you? Pull, will you? pull, can't you? pull, won't you? That's the way you'll get your gold, my lovely fellows! Hurrah for the gold cup of sperm oil, my heroes! Yes, and easy, easy; don't be in a hurry—don't be in a hurry. Why don't you break your oars, you dogs! That's it—that's it; long and strong. Bite on something, you devils! Here!" he said, pulling his knife from his belt, "every mother's son of you, pull out your knife, and put it between your teeth! That's it, my great hearts, my children, that's it! Now you're pulling like something! Now you are strong as that steel blade, my boys!" That is how Stubbs taught his men the religion of rowing. He would say the most terrifying things to his crew, his voice full of fun and fury. But the fury only added to the fun, and in the end they pulled at their oars for the joke of the thing.

16   Starbuck, too, pushed us onward toward the whales. He spoke in a low voice, almost a hissing whisper, so deep was his passion for the hunt. "Strong, boys, strong. There's tubs of sperm oil ahead, and that's what we came for! Pull, my boys—sperm oil's the game. This is our duty and our profit. Duty and profit, hand in hand—pull boys!" Duty and profit: this was Starbuck's religion.

17   Captain Ahab steered his boat ahead of the others. His crew of Manila seamen were as strong as steel and whalebone. In the bow of the boat stood Fedallah, his harpoon ready. In the stern, old Ahab stood ready at the steering oar, as he had done in a thousand boat-lowerings before. All at once, his arm rose into the air in an odd movement and then remained fixed. His five oarsmen stopped pulling. Boat and crew sat still on the sea. Instantly, the three other boats behind Ahab paused on their way. The whales had suddenly and smoothly lowered themselves deeper down into the blue. Only Ahab, closer to

them, had seen their movement. For the moment, the huge whales had disappeared.

II

18   "Every man look out along his oar!" Starbuck called to us. "You, Queequeg, stand up!" Queequeg's heart and harpoon both were ready. He stood up tall in the bow, his eager eyes on the spot where the whales were last seen. Starbuck stood in the stern coolly balancing himself to the rolling boat. Silently, searchingly, he eyed the wide blue eye of the sea.

19   Not very far away from us, Flask's boat lay breathlessly still. Flask stood in the stern, on the narrow top of a strong, thick post used to guide the harpoon ropes when a harpooned whale pulls the boat along behind it. The post was short. Flask, too, was short—small and short. At the same time, he was big and tall in his passion. The post did not satisfy him.

20   "I can't see three waves off. Hold up an oar, there, and let me stand on that."

21   At his chief's word, Daggoo, Flask's huge African harpooner, moved to the stern. "I'm as good an oar as any, Sir," he said. "Will you climb up?"

22   With that, Daggoo planted his feet against the sides of the boat. He held out his hands to help Flask climb. Flask jumped up high and dry on Daggoo's shoulders.

23   "Thank you very much, my fine fellow," said Flask. "Only, I wish you fifty feet taller!"

24   At any time it is a strange sight to see the wonderfully unconscious ability of the whaleman. He can stand balanced in his boat even when the seas are rolling and crashing furiously under his feet. But to see the little Flask atop the tall Daggoo was even stranger. The black man rolled with every roll of the sea, and with the cool, easy, unthinking command of a king. And though chief of the boat, Flask balanced like a snow-flake on Daggoo's broad back. Now and then, Flask would shout, or stamp his foot on Daggoo's shoulder in his eagerness to find the whales. But Daggoo never moved, except with the roll of the sea. So it is with human wishes: We shout and stamp upon the forgiving earth in our passion, but the earth does not change her seas or seasons because of us.

25   Meanwhile, in the third boat, Stubb showed no such far-looking passion as Starbuck and Flask. The whales might be down for a short dive out of fear, or a longer dive to find

food. In either case, Stubb would wait calmly with the aid of his pipe. He pulled it out of his hat-band, where he always wore it like a feather. But he hardly had time to light a match across the rough skin of his hand. Tashtego, Stubb's harpooner, stood with eyes staring to leeward like two fixed stars. Suddenly he dropped down to his seat.

26   "Down, down all, and pull!—There they are!" he cried.

27   No landsman would have sensed the nearness of the whales at that moment. Nothing showed but a troubled bit of greenish water. A thin white fog blew past the waves to leeward. The air around seemed to move, like the air over heated plates of steel. And beneath this troubled pool of air and sea the whales moved onward, faster, faster than the boats could row.

28   "Pull, pull, my good boys," Starbuck called to us in his low-hissed, passionate whisper. He did not say much to his crew, nor did we say much to him. But the silence of the boat was sometimes broken by his strange whispers, now sharp with command, now soft with begging.

29   How different from Starbuck was Flask! "Sing out and roar, my good hearts! Row our boat to the whale's broad back! On, on! Pull, pull!—only get me there, and I will give you my house, my wife, my children. Row on! I will go mad! Look at that white water!" Flask pulled his hat from his head, stamped up and down on it, picked it up, and finally threw it into the rolling sea.

30   "Look at that fellow now," said Stubb philosophically to his own crew. "He's all in a fury! But you, boys, pull smoothly onwards. Happily, happily—sweet pudding for supper, happy's the word. But pull softly—smooth, now—on those oars. Crack your backbones and bite your knives in two! Take it easy, I say, but break your heart and bones!"

31   But what Captain Ahab said to his crew—those words should not be written here. Only the sharks in the terrific sea should give ear to his furious words, or see his eyes full of red murder. So did Ahab race to the hunt.

III

32   The chase was a scene full of quick wonder. The huge waves of the all-powerful sea rolled and roared. The men would take a deep breath as their boat balanced atop a wave sharp enough to cut it in two. Then they would slide down

the other side, the harpooners and crew chiefs shouting, the oarsmen struggling. Then the long hard row up the opposite hill and the terrifying slide again down its other side. And behind the boats the wonderful sight of the *Pequod* following fast, her sails wide to the wind. All this filled, and over-filled, the men's hearts. No one can feel stranger or stronger passion than one who for the first time enters the furious circle of the hunted sperm whale.

33   The dancing white water over the whales was becoming more visible as the clouds darkened. The jets of water and air coming from the whales began to spread out right and left as the whales separated from each other. Our boats pulled further apart, following them.

34   On Starbuck's boat, we had put up our sail. We rushed forward so fast in the rising wind that the leeward oars were almost torn from our hands. As the storm gathered, fog blew down over the waves. Soon we were running through a thick cloud of it and could see neither the big ship *Pequod* nor any of the other small boats.

35   "There's white water again, men," Starbuck whispered. "There's time yet to kill a whale before the storm breaks. Stand up, Queequeg!" Queequeg, harpoon in his hand, stood tall. "There's his back," said Starbuck. "*There, there,* give it to him!"

36   A short, hissing sound leapt out of the boat; it was the pointed steel of Queequeg's harpoon. Then, all in a terrific movement, an unseen push came up under the stern. The bow of the boat seemed to strike a hill. Something rolled and thundered beneath us just as the storm broke overhead. The sail blew apart into pieces. The boat turned, and we were thrown, breathless, into the furious white waves. Storm, whale and harpoon had all mixed together. And the whale, only touched by the steel, escaped.

37   The boat was half filled with water but not broken. Swimming round it, we caught the floating oars, and pulled ourselves back into the boat. There we sat, up to our knees in sea, the water covering every bone and board.

38   Now the wind increased to a roar, and the waves crashed around the boat and into it. Thunder and lightning cracked around us. We shouted to the other boats, but our voices were useless in the rising storm. The fog hid the *Pequod* from us completely.

39   Starbuck struggled with the waterproof matchbox. After many failures he managed to light a tiny lamp. He handed it to Queequeg to tie to the end of his harpoon. There, then, he sat, holding up that foolish candle in the heart of that terrible emptiness. There, then, he sat, through the dark hours of the night, hopelessly holding up hope in the middle of nothingness.

40   Wet to the bone, cold to the heart, we lifted our eyes as morning came on in the dark sky. Fog still lay spread out over the sea. The empty lamp lay broken at the bottom of the boat. Suddenly Queequeg jumped up, holding a hand to his ear. Through the lessening sounds of the storm, we could hear a faint sighing and cracking of ropes and masts in the wind.

41   The sound came nearer and nearer, until the fog was broken by a huge, ghostly form. Terrified, we jumped into the sea as the *Pequod* rose up behind and above us, only a ship's length away. Floating on the waves, we watched as our empty boat was pulled under the *Pequod's* bow, like a wood chip in a waterfall. Then it was gone. We swam hard for the *Pequod*. We were thrown against its side by the crashing waves, but at last were taken up and safely landed on deck.

42   And what of the other whale boats? Before the storm closed in, the other crews had cut lose from their whales and returned to the *Pequod* in good time. They all believed that our crew was lost under the furious waves. But still they sailed nearby, thinking to find a sign of our passing—a lonely oar, perhaps, floating on the endless sea.

AFTER YOU READ THE STORY

A. Understanding the Plot

Answer the following questions with complete sentences.

1. What is the weather like at the start of the story? What are the crew members doing?
2. What does the lookout call out to the men, and why?
3. What do the men do in response to the lookout's call?

4　What happens to the boat Ishmael is in after Queequeg throws his harpoon at the whale? What happens to the crew? What happens to the whale?

5. The morning after the storm, Ishmael's boat has another adventure. What is it? Where are the men at the very end of the story?

B. Close Reading

Part I (pages 87–91)

The sailors and harpooners on the *Pequod* come from many different places in the world. Match the name of the crewman with the part of the world he comes from.

1. __d__ Tashtego   a. Africa
2. __e__ Fedallah   b. Manila
3. __a__ Daggoo   c. Polynesia
4. __c__ Queequeg   d. Martha's Vineyard Island
5. __b__ Ahab's boat crew   e. the East Asian islands

Part II (pages 91–92)

The following sentences tell us about the four crew chiefs. Write the name of the crew chief in front of the sentence or sentences that describe his personality, situation, or actions.

The four crew chiefs: Ahab, Stubb, Starbuck, and Flask.

_____ 1. He is mostly strong and silent, but he speaks in a passionate whisper.

_____ 2. To see the whales, he stands on the back of his harpooner.

_____ 3. He becomes so excited that he throws his hat into the sea.

_____ 4. His harpooner first sees the whales come back up to the surface.

_____ 5. He is a small man with a large passion for the hunt.

_____ 6. He hunts with murder in his eyes.

_____ 7. He smokes his pipe quietly while he waits for the whales to "blow" again.

Part III (pages 92–95)

The events of the hunt happen quickly. Melville succeeds in creating a scene of great excitement and confusion. We can understand exactly what happened only by rereading carefully. Put numbers in the blank spaces next to the ten sentences below to show the order in which the events take place in the story.

The first and the last are done for you.

_____ a. They wait all night for help, Queequeg holding high a little lamp.

_____ b. The clouds darken, the whales separate, and the boats pull apart from each other.

_____ c. Starbuck tells his men that there's time to catch a whale before the storm breaks.

_____ d. The *Pequod* suddenly appears through the fog just behind them, and the men jump from the boat into the sea.

__1__ e. All the boats chase after the whales, rowing up one side of the huge waves and sliding down the other side.

_____ f. The storm breaks and a whale hits the boat from below, turning it over into the sea.

_____ g. As the storm gathers, Starbuck's boat is separated from the others in the fog.

__10__ h. Starbuck's crew is taken safely onto the deck of the *Pequod*.

_____ i. The men climb back into their little boat, which is half filled with water.

_____ j. Queequeg throws his harpoon at a whale.

C. Vocabulary Practice

Melville's vocabulary is rich in words that make us feel excitement, adventure, or danger. Complete the sentences with the words below.

eager	instantly	passion
fury	hiss	terrifying

1. Tashtego's cry of "There she blows!" was a call to action, and the crew of the *Pequod* responded _____.

2. After the boats were lowered from the *Pequod* into the sea, the _____ men jumped like goats from the deck down into them.

3. Stubb tried to get his crew to row harder by saying the most _____ things to them. But his voice showed no anger or hatred; it was filled with fun rather than _____.

4. Starbuck's voice is strange, too, but very different from Stubb's. His voice sounds like a sharp _____, almost a whisper.

5. Like the other crew chiefs, Flask has a _____ for the hunt, and his small size seems only to increase it.

D. Word Forms

Noun	Verb	Adjective	Adverb
fury	infuriate	furious	furiously
laziness	laze	lazy	lazily
passion	impassion	passionate	passionately
satisfaction	satisfy	satisfying	satisfyingly
terror	terrify	terrifying	terrifyingly

Using the chart above, choose the correct forms of the words to complete the following sentences.

1. (*fury*) Ahab's quietly murderous eyes showed ____fury____, but Flask's ____furious____ jumping up and down showed his passion for the hunt.

2. (*laziness*) The men ____lazed____ around the deck until Tashtego sighted the whales; and at that moment their ____laziness____ instantly disappeared.

بيّن

3. (*passion*) All the crew chiefs were <u>passionate</u> about the whale hunt, but each showed his <u>passio</u> in a different way.

4. (*satisfaction*) Flask got no <u>satisfaction</u> from standing on the post; but standing on Daggoo's back finally <u>satisfied</u> him.

5. (*terror*) The storm winds blew the waves to a <u>terrifying</u> height, but the men felt excitement rather than <u>terror</u>.

E. Language Activity: Imagery

Imagery is the use of language that gives the reader a clear picture (image) of what the author is trying to describe. Read the following quotations from the story carefully, then choose the word or phrase that best expresses what the underlined image helps us to understand.

Example:

The *Pequod* "sailed smoothly over the <u>lead-gray</u> sea." (paragraph 1) The image helps us to understand
a. the heaviness of the sea's waves
b. the darkness of the sea
c. the sea's worthlessness (compared to silver or gold)

1. The eager crews "jumped <u>goat-like</u> from the high deck" to the boats below. (paragraph 12) The image helps us to understand
   a. the stupidity of the sailors
   b. the danger to those in the boats below
   c. how quick and sure-footed the men were

2. The Manila seamen of Ahab's boat crew are compared to "<u>steel and whalebone</u>." (paragraph 17) The image helps us to understand
   a. the strength of those men
   b. the men's strong interest in harpoons and whales
   c. how straight the men stood

3. While waiting for the whales to surface, "Flask's boat lay breathlessly still." (paragraph 19) The image helps us to understand
   a. how difficult it is to breathe in a boat that's not moving
   b. how near sleep the men in the boat were
   c. the close attention the men were paying to the sea

4. To look for whales, Flask climbed up and "balanced like a snow-flake on Daggoo's broad back." (paragraph 24) The image helps us to understand
   a. Flask's whiteness against the African's darkness
   b. Flask's smallness and lightness compared with his huge harpooner
   c. both of the above

5. Looking for the whales, Tashtego "stood with eyes staring to leeward like two fixed stars." (paragraph 25) The image helps us to understand
   a. how hard Tashtego was staring
   b. how far away Tashtego's mind was
   c. how warm Tashtego's eyes were

6. During the chase, "the men would take a deep breath as their boat balanced atop a wave sharp enough to cut it in two." (paragraph 32) The image helps us to understand
   a. the shape of the waves
   b. the solid strength of the boat
   c. the hardness of the sea's water

7. As the men felt a huge push under the stern, "the bow of the boat seemed to strike a hill." (paragraph 36) The image helps us to understand
   a. how high the waves were above them
   b. how big and solid the whale felt below them
   c. how like land the sea was all around them

F. Discussion: Personal Opinions

1. Which of the characters in this story did you like most? Why? Which did you like least? Why?
2. What kinds of stories or films or plays do you prefer: adventure stories? philosophical stories? love stories? historical stories? political stories? family stories? a mixture of one or more of those? another kind not mentioned? Why?

3. What made it possible for people from so many different places to live peacefully with each other on the *Pequod*? What made it necessary?

4. In your own world, why do people from different places find it difficult to live peacefully with each other? What are the things that make it possible or necessary for them to live in peace?

G. Writing: Ishmael's Diary

You are Ishmael. You have been keeping a diary of your experiences at sea. The past two days of the whale hunt have given you more than usual to write about. You want to summarize the main events of the hunt in a short space; that is, you want to write a summary. Using the phrases below as a guide, write down in your own words what happened during the whale hunt.

Date: May 3, 1848
Location: Northwest of the Azores

- Weather:
- Tashtego sights the whales
- How the crew responded
- Chasing the whales . . . they dive and disappear . . .
- Changes in the weather while we wait for the whales to surface
- What happened when they came up again . . .
- Why our boat kept chasing the whales
- Queequeg throws his harpoon, and then . . .
- What happened during the night
- What happened the next morning

7

PASTE

❋

Adapted from the story by
HENRY JAMES

Henry James was born in 1843 in Washington Place, New York. His father was a well-known religious thinker; his older brother, William James, became a famous philosopher. James was educated in New York and Europe and attended Harvard Law School. His years of school in London, Paris, and Geneva gave him a love for Europe. He traveled often to Europe, and after 1876 he made his home in London. James wrote widely. In addition to plays, criticism, and short stories, he wrote about twenty novels. *The Europeans*, *Washington Square*, *The Portrait of a Lady*, and *The Bostonians* are among the best known. Much of James's work deals with the contrast in values and behavior of Americans and Europeans. He became a British citizen shortly before his death in 1916.

BEFORE YOU READ THE STORY

A. About the Author

Read the paragraph about Henry James on page 103. Write down at least three reasons why (in your opinion) a person might want to change his or her citizenship. Do any of them seem to fit Henry James?

B. The Pictures

Look at the pictures on pages 108 and 113. One object and one person are common to both pictures. What are they?

C. Thinking About False Jewels, False People

The word *paste* in the title of the story has a special meaning. It can mean the soft mixture used to glue paper or to brush your teeth, but here it means a mixture used to make artificial (false, not real) jewelry. The story is about jewels, real or false, and qualities in people's characters that might also be called real or false. What are some of the qualities that people often show to the outside world that are not real, but false?

D. Scanning Different Sources of Information

For this exercise you will need to use the paragraphs about Willa Cather (page 49), Susan Glaspell (page 67), Herman Melville (page 85), and Henry James (page 103).

Sometimes we need to find small bits of information from several different pieces of writing. In order to find the information asked for in the questions below, let your eyes move quickly over the four paragraphs mentioned above until you find the dates or places or words that allow you to answer the question. Try to complete the exercise in less than ten minutes.

1. Which of the writers was born first?
2. Which of the writers died last?
3. Where was each writer born?
4. Which writer lived on a farm as a child?
5. Which writer attended law school?
6. Which of the writers can you match with the following subjects: Europe, the sea, pioneers, Provincetown Playhouse?

KEY WORDS   *Is she too honest?*

Charlotte, the main character in "Paste," is a **governess;** she lives in the home of a wealthy family, teaching and training the children. As the story begins, Charlotte has taken a few days' leave from her work to go to the **funeral** of a stepaunt who recently died. During her visit with her uncle's family, Charlotte discusses with her cousin Arthur a **pearl necklace** that belonged to her aunt. This piece of jewelry, the key to the story, raises questions about certain **virtues** (honesty, goodness, purity), or their opposite (especially **greed,** the passionate desire for things of value), in all the story's characters.

a little bit foolish!

Naive innocent

maternity / leave
military /
fake / love
jewelry
laugh
promise
Name
adress

woman's role
- Nurse
- teacher
- cook
- governess
- tutor

letter of recommendation

heirloom

PASTE

I

"I've found a lot more of her things," Charlotte's cousin said to her after his stepmother's funeral. "They're up in her room—but they're things I wish *you'd* look at."

2   Charlotte and her cousin, Arthur Prime, were waiting for lunch in the garden of Arthur's father, who had been a country minister. It seemed to Charlotte that Arthur's face showed the wish to express some kind of feeling. It was not surprising that Arthur should feel something. His stepmother had recently died, only three weeks after his father's death.

3   Charlotte had no money of her own and lived with a wealthy family as governess for their children. She had asked for leave to attend the funeral. During her stay Charlotte had noticed that her cousin seemed somehow to grieve without sorrow, to suffer without pain. It was Arthur's habit to drop a comment and leave her to pick it up without help. What "things" did he mean now? However, since she hoped for a remembrance of her stepaunt, she went to look at these "things" he had spoken of.

4   As she entered the darkened room, Charlotte's eyes were struck by the bright jewels that glowed on the table. Even before touching them, she guessed they were things of the theater. They were much too fine to have been things of a minister's wife. Her stepaunt had worn no jewelry to speak of, and these were crowns and necklaces, diamonds and gold. After her first shock, Charlotte picked them up. They seemed like proof of the far-off, faded story of her stepaunt's life. Her uncle, a country minister, had lost his first wife. With a small son, Arthur, and a large admiration for the theater, he had developed an even larger admiration for an unknown actress. He had offered his hand in marriage. Still more surprisingly, the actress had accepted. Charlotte had suspected for years that her stepaunt's acting could not have brought her either fame or fortune.

5   "You see what it is—old stuff of the time she never liked to mention."

6   Charlotte jumped a little. Arthur must have followed her upstairs. He was watching her slightly nervous recognition of the jewelry.

7   "I thought so myself," she replied. Then, to show intelligence without sounding silly, she said, "How odd they look!"

8   "They look awful," said Arthur Prime. "Cheap glass diamonds as big as potatoes. Actors have better taste now."

9   "Oh," said Charlotte, wanting to sound as knowledgeable as he, "now actresses have real diamonds."

10   "Some of them do."

11   "Oh, I mean even the bad ones—the nobodies, too."

12   Arthur replied coldly, "Some of the nobodies have the biggest jewels. But Mama wasn't *that* sort of actress."

13   "A nobody?" Charlotte asked.

14   "She wasn't a nobody that someone would give—well, not a nobody with diamonds. This stuff is worthless."

15   There was something about the old theater pieces that attracted Charlotte. She continued to turn them over in her hands.

16   Arthur paused, then he asked: "Do you care for them? I mean, as a remembrance?"

17   "Of you?" Charlotte said quickly.

18   "Of me? What do I have to do with it? Of your poor, dead aunt, who was so kind to you," he said virtuously.

19 "Well, I would rather have them than nothing."

20 "Then please take them." His face expressed more hope than generosity.

21 "Thank you." Charlotte lifted two or three pieces up and then set them down again. They were light, but so large and false that they made an awkward gift.

22 "Did you know she had kept them?"

23 "I don't believe she knew they were there, and I'm sure my father didn't. Her connection with the theater was over. These things were just put in a corner and forgotten."

24 Charlotte wondered, "What corner had she found to put them in?"

25 "She hadn't *found* it, she'd lost it," Arthur insisted. "The whole thing had passed from her mind after she put the stuff into a box in the schoolroom cupboard. The box had been stuck there for years."

26 "Are you sure they're not worth anything?" Charlotte asked dreamily.

27 But Arthur Prime had already asked himself this question and found the answer.

28 "If they had been worth anything, she would have sold them long ago. Unfortunately, my father and she were never wealthy enough to keep things of value locked up."

29 He looked at Charlotte for agreement and added, like one who is unfamiliar with generosity, "And if they're worth anything at all—why, you're all the more welcome to them."

30 Charlotte picked up a small silk bag. As she opened it she answered him, "I shall like them. They're all I have."

31 "All you have—?"

32 "That belonged to her."

33 He looked around the poor room as if to question her greed. "Well, what else do you want?"

34 "Nothing. Thank you very much." As she said this she looked into the small silk bag. It held a necklace of large pearls.

35 "Perhaps this is worth something. Feel it." She passed him the necklace.

36 He weighed it in his hands without interest. "Worthless, I'm sure—it's paste."

37 "But *is* it paste?"

38 He spoke impatiently. "Pearls nearly as large as nuts?"

39 "But they're heavy," Charlotte insisted.

40   "No heavier than anything else," he said, as if amused at her simplicity.

41   Charlotte studied them a little, feeling them, turning them around.

42   "Couldn't they possibly be real?"

43   "Of that size? Put away with that stuff?"

44   "Well, I admit it's not likely," Charlotte said. "And pearls are so easily imitated."

45   "Pearls are *not* easily imitated, to anyone who knows about them. These have no shine. Anyway, how would she have got them?"

46   "Couldn't they have been a present?" Charlotte asked.

47   Arthur looked at her as if she had said something improper. "You mean because actresses are approached by men who—" He stopped suddenly. "No, they couldn't have been a present," he said sharply, and left the room.

48   Later, in the evening, they met to discuss Charlotte's departure the next day. At the end of the conversation, Arthur said,

49   "I really can't let you think that my stepmother was at *any* time of her life a woman who could—"

50   "Accept expensive presents from admirers?" Charlotte added. Somehow Arthur always made her speak more directly than she meant to. But he only answered, seriously,

51   "Exactly."

52   "I didn't think of that, when I spoke this morning," said Charlotte apologetically, "but I see what you mean."

53   "I mean that her virtue was above question," said Arthur Prime.

54   "A hundred times yes."

55   "Therefore she could never have afforded such pearls on her small salary."

56   "Of *course* she couldn't," Charlotte answered comfortingly. "Anyway," she continued, "I noticed that the clasp that holds the pearls together isn't even gold. I suppose it wouldn't be, with false pearls."

57   "The whole thing is cheap paste," Arthur announced, as if to end their discussion. "If the pearls were *real*, and she had hidden them all these years—"

58   "Yes?" asked Charlotte curiously.

59   "Well, I wouldn't know *what* to think!"

60   "Oh, I see," said Charlotte, and their conversation ended.

II

61   When she was back at work again, the false jewels seemed silly to Charlotte. She wasn't sure why she had taken them. She put them away under a pile of clothing, and there they might have stayed, except for the arrival of Mrs. Guy.

62   Mrs. Guy was a strange little woman with red hair and black dresses. She had the face of a baby, but took command like a general. She was a friend of the family Charlotte worked for. She had come to organize a week of parties to celebrate the 21st birthday of the family's oldest son. She happily accepted Charlotte's help with the entertainments.

63   "Tomorrow and Thursday are all right, but we need to plan something for Friday evening," she announced to Charlotte.

64   "What would you like to do?"

65   "Well, plays are my strong point, you know," said Mrs. Guy.

66   They discussed plays and looked at the hats and dresses they might wear.

67   "But we need something to brighten these up," Mrs. Guy decided. "These things are too dull. Haven't you got anything else?"

68   "Well, I do have a few things . . ." Charlotte admitted slowly. She went to find the jewels for Mrs. Guy. "Perhaps they're too bright, they're just glass and paste."

69   "Larger than life!" Mrs. Guy was excited. "They are just what we need. They'll give me great ideas!"

70   The next morning she came to find Charlotte in the schoolroom.

71   "I don't understand where you got these pieces," she said to Charlotte.

72   "They belonged to my aunt, who died a few months ago. She was an actress for several years. They were part of her theatrical equipment."

73   "She left them to you?"

74   "No; my cousin, her stepson, who naturally has no use for them, gave them to me as a remembrance of her. She was a dear, kind person, always so nice to me, and I was very fond of her."

75   Mrs. Guy listened with interest. "But it must be your *cousin* who is a 'dear, kind person.' Is *he* also 'always so nice' to you?"

76   "What do you mean?" asked Charlotte.

77   "Can't you guess?"

78   A strange feeling came over Charlotte. "The pearls—" she started to say.

79   "Doesn't your cousin know either?"

80   Charlotte felt herself turning pink. "They're *not* paste?"

81   "Haven't you looked at them?" Mrs. Guy continued.

82   Charlotte felt ashamed. Not to have known that the pearls were real!

83   "Come to my room when you finish teaching," Mrs. Guy ordered, "You'll see!"

84   Later, in Mrs. Guy's room, Charlotte stared at the pearls around Mrs. Guy's neck. Surely they were the only mysterious thing her stepaunt had owned.

85   "What in the world have you done to them?"

86   "I only handled them, understood them, admired them and put them on," Mrs. Guy answered proudly. "That's what pearls need. They need to be worn—it wakes them up. They're alive, you see. How have these been treated? They must have been buried, ignored. They were half dead. Don't you *know* about pearls?"

87   "How could I have known?" said penniless Charlotte. "Do you?"

88   "I know everything about pearls. These were simply asleep. From the moment I touched them you could see they were real."

89   "I couldn't see," admitted Charlotte, "although I did wonder about them. Then their value—"

90   "Oh, their value is excellent!"

91   Charlotte felt dizzy. "But my cousin didn't know. He thinks they're worthless."

92   "Because the rest of the jewels are false? Then your cousin is a fool. But, anyway, he gave them to you."

93   "But if he gave them to me because he thought they were worthless—"

94   "You think you must give them back? I don't agree. If he was such a fool that he didn't recognize their value, it's his fault."

95   Charlotte looked at the pearls. They *were* beautiful. At

the moment, however, they seemed to belong more to Mrs. Guy than to Charlotte *or* her cousin. She said finally:

96   "Yes, he insisted that the pearls were paste, even after I clearly said they looked different from the other things."

97   "Well, then, you see!" said Mrs. Guy. Her voice expressed more than victory over Arthur Prime—she sounded relieved.

98   But Charlotte was still not sure. "You see, he thought they couldn't be different because they shouldn't be."

99   "Shouldn't be? I don't understand."

100   "Well, how would she have got them?" Charlotte asked directly.

101   "Do you mean she might have stolen them?"

102   "No, but she had been an actress."

103   "Well, then!" cried Mrs. Guy. "That's exactly how she got them."

104   "Yes, but she wasn't famous or rich."

105   "Was she ugly?" Mrs. Guy inquired.

106   "No. She must have looked rather nice when she was young."

107   "Well, then!" cried Mrs. Guy again, as if she had proved her point.

108   "You mean the pearls were a present? That's just the idea my cousin dislikes—that she had such a generous admirer."

109   "And that she wouldn't have taken the pearls for nothing? I should think not! Let's hope she gave him *something* in return. Let's hope she was kind to him."

110   "Well," Charlotte continued, "I suppose she must have been 'kind' as you call it. That's why none of us knew she had something so valuable. That's why she had to hide them."

111   "You're suggesting that she was ashamed of them?"

112   "Well, she had married a minister."

113   "But he married *her*. What did he think of her past life?"

114   "Well, that she was not the sort of woman who encouraged such gifts."

115   "Ah! my dear! What woman is *not*!" said Mrs. Guy with a smile.

116   "And I don't want to give away her secret," continued Charlotte. "I liked her very much."

117	"Then don't!" decided Mrs. Guy. "Keep them."
118	"It's so difficult!" sighed Charlotte. "I must think. I'll tell you tonight, after I decide what to do."
119	"But may I wear them—this evening at dinner?" Mrs. Guy's hands held the pearls lovingly.
120	It was probably Mrs. Guy's possessiveness that decided Charlotte; but for the moment she only said, "As you like," before she left the room.
121	It was almost eleven o'clock before Charlotte had a chance to meet with Mrs. Guy again that evening. Mrs. Guy had worn the pearls to dinner, and announced that they had been "A great success, my dear, a sensation!"
122	"They *are* beautiful," Charlotte agreed, "but I can't be silent."
123	"Then you plan to return them?"
124	"If I don't, I'll be a thief."
125	"If you do, you're a fool!" said Mrs. Guy angrily.
126	"Well, of the two . . ." Charlotte answered faintly.
127	Mrs. Guy interrupted her. "You won't tell him I told you that they're real, will you?"
128	"No, certainly not."
129	"Then, perhaps he won't believe you, and he will give them back to us!" And feeling much better, Mrs. Guy went to bed.
130	But Charlotte didn't like to return the pearls to Arthur Prime by mail, and was too busy to go to town herself. On the last day of Mrs. Guy's visit, she came to Charlotte.
131	"Come now, how much will you sell them for?"
132	"The pearls? Oh, you'll have to bargain with my cousin."
133	"Where does he live?"
134	Charlotte gave her the address.
135	"But how can I talk with him if you don't do anything about returning them?" Mrs. Guy complained.
136	"Oh, I *will*. I'm only waiting until the family goes to town. Do you want the pearls so much?"
137	"I'm dying for them. There's a special mystery about them. They have a white glow." Mrs. Guy paused. "My dear," she whispered, "they're things of love!"
138	"Oh, dear!" cried Charlotte.
139	"They're things of passion!"
140	"Oh, heavens!"

III

141   Mrs. Guy left, but Charlotte couldn't forget her words. She felt she had a new view of her dear, dead aunt. Had her stepaunt suffered over the pearls, hidden away with the false jewels? Charlotte began wearing the pearls in private; she came to feel a strange attachment to them. But still she was poor, and she dreamed that Arthur Prime might show an uncharacteristic generosity and say to her:

142   "Oh, keep the pearls! Of course, I couldn't afford to give them to you if I had known their value. But since you *have* got them, and found out the truth yourself, I really can't take them away from you."

143   In fact, his reaction was quite different when she finally went to town to tell him her story.

144   "I don't believe in them," he said. He was angry and pale.

145   "That's exactly what I wanted to hear," Charlotte replied.

146   "It's a most unpleasant, improper suggestion," he added. "To think that she . . ."

147   "If you're afraid to believe they're real, it's not my fault."

148   Arthur said nothing for a while. Then he picked them up. "They're what I said originally. They're only paste."

149   "Then may I keep them?"

150   "No. I want a better opinion."

151   "Better than your opinion."

152   "No. Better than *yours*." Arthur took the pearls and locked them in a drawer.

153   "You say I'm afraid," he added. "But I won't be afraid to take them to a jeweler to ask for an opinion."

154   "And if he says they're real?"

155   "He won't say so. He couldn't," Arthur insisted.

156   Two weeks later Charlotte received a letter about the pearls from Arthur. Still later Mrs. Guy was invited to dinner by Charlotte's employer. She was wearing a beautiful string of pearls.

157   "Do you see?" She came over to greet Charlotte, pointing at her necklace.

158   Charlotte wore a sickly smile. "They're almost as nice as Arthur's," she said.

159   "Almost? Where are your eyes, my dear? They *are* Arthur's. I tracked them to the jeweler's window where he sold them."

160   "*Sold* them?" Charlotte was horrified. "He wrote me that I had insulted his stepmother and that the jeweler had shown him that he was right—he said the pearls were only paste!"

161   Mrs. Guy stared at her. "Ah, I told you he wouldn't believe you."

162   "He wrote me," Charlotte continued, full of her private wrong, "that he had smashed them."

163   "He is really very disturbed." Mrs. Guy's voice expressed pity and wonder.

164   But it was not quite clear whom she pitied, Arthur or Charlotte. And Charlotte felt disturbed, too, when she thought about it later. Had Mrs. Guy really tracked the pearls to a jeweler's window? Or had she dealt with Arthur directly? Charlotte remembered clearly that she had given Mrs. Guy his address.

[handwritten: Pearls. she 5_ she finds a necklace of large wonders if the pearls are possibly real.]

AFTER YOU READ THE STORY

[handwritten: 6 - "to have skeleton in your closet"]

A. Understanding the Plot

Answer the following questions with complete sentences.

1. Who has recently died?
2. What does Arthur ask Charlotte to do?
3. What are the "things" that Charlotte finds in her stepaunt's room? Describe them. *[handwritten: costume jewelry]*
4. Why did Arthur's stepmother have these things?
5. What does Charlotte find in the small silk bag? What does she wonder about what she has found?
6. What does Arthur do with the jewelry? Why is he sure the jewelry is not real?
7. Why does Charlotte show the jewelry to Mrs. Guy?
8. What does Mrs. Guy tell Charlotte about the pearls?
9. What does Charlotte decide to do with the pearls?
10. What does Arthur tell Charlotte the jeweler said about the pearls?
11. In the end, where does Mrs. Guy say she got the pearls? Where else may she have got them?

Part I (pages 105–109)

In Part I of the story, Henry James gives us many clues to what causes Charlotte and Arthur to behave as they do. Explore their characters by answering the following questions about them.

1. Charlotte
   a. What is Charlotte's situation in life—that is, what work does she do, and why does she do it?
   b. Which of the following words best describes Charlotte's character: *distrustful, thoughtful, playful*? Choose a sentence or more from the first two pages of the story to prove your point.
   c. Does Charlotte seem eager to find fault or eager to please? Support your answer with quotations from the conversation between Charlotte and Arthur in paragraphs 5–60.

2. Arthur
   a. What was Arthur's father's profession? What was Arthur's stepmother's profession before she married his father? How does Arthur feel about his stepmother?
   b. What do the following quotations from the story tell about Arthur's character?

   . . . Charlotte had noticed that her cousin seemed somehow to grieve without sorrow, to suffer without pain. (paragraph 3)

   He looked at Charlotte for agreement and added, like one who is unfamiliar with generosity, "And if they're worth anything at all—why, you're all the more welcome to them." (paragraph 29)

   c. Arthur is sure the jewels are false. More important, he *needs to be sure* they are false. Why? Study the following quotations before you answer.

   Mama wasn't that *sort of actress.* (paragraph 12)

   "No, they couldn't have been a present," he said sharply, and left the room. (paragraph 47)

   I mean that her virtue was above question. (paragraph 53)

   If the pearls were real, *and she had hidden them all these years. . . . Well, I wouldn't know what to think!* (paragraphs 57 and 59)

Part II (pages 110–114)

Like any speakers having a real conversation, Charlotte and Mrs. Guy leave part of their meaning unsaid, knowing that the other person will understand. Read the following quotations and answer the questions about their unspoken meanings.

1. *Mrs. Guy listened with interest. "But it must be your cousin who is a 'dear, kind person.' Is he 'always so nice' to you?"*
   "What do you mean?" asked Charlotte. (paragraphs 75, 76)

   What *does* Mrs. Guy mean? What does Mrs. Guy know about the pearls that Charlotte only suspects? Why does Mrs. Guy think that Arthur has been kind to Charlotte?

2. *"But if he gave them to me because he thought they were worthless—"* (paragraph 93)

   Mrs. Guy knows exactly what Charlotte is thinking. What is it? If the pearls are real, what does Charlotte think she should do with them, and why?

3. *"Yes, [said Charlotte,] he insisted that the pearls were paste, even after I clearly said they looked different from the other things."*
   "Well, then, you see!" said Mrs. Guy. (paragraphs 96, 97)

   With these words—"Well, then, you see!"—Mrs. Guy tells Charlotte what she should do with the pearls. What is that?

4. *"Do you mean she might have stolen them?"*
   "No, but she had been an actress."
   "Well, then!" cried Mrs. Guy. "That's exactly how she got them." (paragraphs 101–103)

   What is Mrs. Guy trying to say? How does she think Charlotte's aunt got the pearls?

5. *"My dear," she [Mrs. Guy] whispered, "they're things of love!"*
   "Oh, dear!" cried Charlotte.
   "They're things of passion!"
   "Oh, heavens!" (paragraphs 137–140)

   With the phrases "Oh, dear!" and "Oh, heavens!" Charlotte says a lot to Mrs. Guy (and to us). What does she think about what Mrs. Guy is suggesting? Why?

6. *"I don't believe in them," he said.*
   "That's exactly what I wanted to hear."
   "It's a most unpleasant, improper suggestion," he added.
   "To think that she . . ." (paragraphs 144–146)

Arthur "doesn't believe in them"—that is, he doesn't believe the pearls are real. Why, for Charlotte, is that "exactly what I wanted to hear"? And why does Arthur think that the idea of the pearls being real is "a most unpleasant, improper suggestion"?

C. Vocabulary Practice

Choose the word that best completes each of the following sentences. All the words appear in "Paste," and the paragraphs in which they first appear are given. If you are uncertain of a word's meaning, you can check its context in the story.

1. I could not quite identify the people in the old photograph, for it was too
   a. disturbed (paragraph 163)
   b. faded (paragraph 4)
   c. awkward (paragraph 21)

2. "I really hated to miss your wonderful party," she said
   a. impatiently (paragraph 38)
   b. virtuously (paragraph 18)
   c. apologetically (paragraph 52)

3. Frank wasn't sure whether his new play was really good or not; he needed to get an audience's
   a. reaction (paragraph 143)
   b. sensation (paragraph 121)
   c. fame (paragraph 4)

4. After he finally admitted stealing the car, he sounded
   a. ignored (paragraph 86)
   b. relieved (paragraph 97)
   c. dizzy (paragraph 91)

5. The carpet seller and Mrs. Haggle drank a friendly cup of tea together and then began seriously to
   a. grieve (paragraph 3)
   b. bargain (paragraph 132)
   c. announce (paragraph 63)

6. The little boy would not let his new truck out of his hands even once during the whole afternoon, again and again showing his
   a. opinion (paragraph 150)
   b. greed (paragraph 33)
   c. possessiveness (paragraph 120)

D. Word Forms

Noun	Verb	Adjective	Adverb
admission	admit	admitted	admittedly
apology	apologize	apologetic	apologetically
disturbance	disturb	disturbing	disturbingly
possession	possess	possessive	possessively
relief	relieve	relieved	

Choose the one form of the word given that correctly completes the following sentences.

1. *(apologize)* Whatever Mrs. Guy said to Charlotte about her possession of the necklace, she did not say it at all _____.

2. *(admit)* No _____ came from Mrs. Guy that her possession of the pearls was in any way wrong or even selfish.

3. *(relieve)* _____ showed clearly in Mrs. Guy's face and voice when Charlotte told her what Arthur had said about the pearls being paste.

4. *(possess)* At first, Arthur seemed more _____ of his stepmother's good name than of the pearls themselves.

5. *(disturb)* The fact that Arthur had lied was _____ to Charlotte, but perhaps not really news to Mrs. Guy.

E. Language Activity: Overstatement

Sometimes a writer describes a character or situation using words that *overstate* the truth—that enlarge the truth in order to make a point. (Examples: *He's bigger than a barn. She eats like a bird.*) Read the following sentences and answer the questions.

1. *She [Mrs. Guy] had the face of a baby, but took command like a general.* (paragraph 62)

Clearly, Mrs. Guy is neither a baby nor a general. James has used overstatement to give the reader a picture of Mrs. Guy. What strangeness in her character does he suggest by combining the words *baby* and *general* in his description of her? Describe Mrs. Guy using your own words. What does she look like? How does she behave with other people?

2. *"Larger than life!" Mrs. Guy was excited. "They are just what we need. They'll give me great ideas!"* (paragraph 69) Here, Mrs. Guy's overstatement tells us about her reaction to the jewels. What does *larger than life* mean? Why will this give Mrs. Guy "great ideas"?

3. *"They* [the pearls] *need to be worn—it wakes them up. They're alive, you see. How have these been treated? They must have been buried, ignored. They were half dead. Don't you* know *about pearls?"* (paragraph 86) Mrs. Guy here talks about the pearls in terms of sleeping and waking, life and death. What, in her opinion, has happened to the pearls since Charlotte lent them to her? How or why did it happen? With her overstatements here, what general point is Mrs. Guy making about pearls?

F. Discussion: The Ending of "Paste"

Henry James fills the final pages of "Paste" with interesting possibilities and leaves the reader to choose among them. The following questions point out some of these possibilities. What is your opinion? With one or more partners, discuss *one* of the three topics. What conclusions do you reach? Report to the whole group.

1. Charlotte finally takes the pearls back to Arthur. She hopes he will let her keep them. Instead, he locks them in a drawer and says he will take them to a jeweler. Yet he says he is sure the jeweler will say they are false. Why, then, does he keep them? Why doesn't he let Charlotte keep them, if he's so sure?

2. When Mrs. Guy learns from Charlotte about Arthur's letter, she expresses "pity and wonder." We are told, however, that "it was not quite clear whom she pitied, Arthur or Charlotte." What reasons might she have for pitying Arthur? What reasons might she have for pitying Charlotte?

3. What do you think about Arthur, finally? Consider: If Mrs. Guy "dealt directly" with him, and if until that moment Arthur really believed he was a virtuous and honest man, then what is he feeling about himself at the end of the story? And what do you feel about him? Were his actions influenced by what he had learned about his stepmother? Do you pity him? Are you amused by what has happened to him? Do you have a low opinion of him?

G. Writing: A Letter to Arthur

Arthur has written a letter to Charlotte about the pearls (see paragraphs 156–162). He says in it that the pearls were definitely false and that Charlotte has insulted his stepmother. He says that he has smashed the pearls. Later, when Charlotte sees Mrs. Guy wearing the pearls, she knows Arthur's letter was a lie. But what is the truth? Did Arthur take the pearls to a jeweler? Did Mrs. Guy buy the pearls from the jeweler? Did she "deal directly" with Arthur? Is she telling lies, too?

Imagine that you are Charlotte. What do you feel about all this? What should you do about it? Write a letter back to Arthur. Express yourself openly and honestly. Tell Arthur what you know and what you suspect. Decide what you think Arthur should do now, and tell him that. Decide what action you will take if Arthur does nothing, and tell him that, too. End the letter:

Very truly yours,

Your cousin, Charlotte

THE LOST PHOEBE

❋

Adapted from the story by
THEODORE DREISER

Theodore Dreiser was born in 1871. When he was a child, his family was poor—so poor, in fact, that his mother and father had to separate from each other in order to support the children. With his mother and two of his sisters, Dreiser lived in many different towns and states. Although he spent only one year at college, Dreiser became a journalist and magazine editor. His first novel, *Sister Carrie*, was published in 1901. The book was not well liked at first, partly because the "good" men in the story were not always rewarded nor the "bad" men always punished. Dreiser was one of the leaders of the "naturalist" school in American writing. He tried to record with great honesty and accuracy exactly what he saw. His writing was not always beautiful on the surface, but its depth was recognized from the beginning. Dreiser's most famous novel was *An American Tragedy*, published in 1925. Dreiser died in 1945.

BEORE YOU READ THE STORY

A. About the Author

The paragraph about Theodore Dreiser on page 123 mentions two important facts about his childhood. What were they? How would you expect these experiences to influence his writing?

B. The Pictures

1. Look at the picture on page 127. What can you tell about the people who live here? What is their home like? In what sort of place is this home?
2. Look at the picture on page 137. Where is the man walking? What time of day is it? What do you notice about his appearance? What conclusions do you draw from the way he looks?

C. Thinking About Country Ways

In this story Dreiser writes about a family in a small country community a century ago. Most people in such communities kept small farms then. Their lives followed a certain pattern according to their work. There wasn't much time, money, or opportunity for making changes in lifestyle. What effect would this have on how people lived? on their relationship to their neighbors? on how people expected them to behave? Have things changed today? Do most country people do the same work, or hold the same job, all their lives? Are they close to their neighbors? Do they expect, or allow, a wide difference in personality and behavior?

D. Skimming for the Basic Idea and Scanning for Information

Sometimes we skim a lengthy piece of writing in order to get the basic idea of the whole piece, and then scan to find specific information. We may or may not need, or want, to return to the beginning and read with care all the way through. In this exercise, you are asked to skim and scan the story of "The Lost Phoebe" and answer questions on the story's basic idea.

1. **Skim** (Try to skim in five minutes or less.)
   a. Read the first sentence or two of each paragraph throughout the story. Read no more than that, but do not rush.
   b. When you come to a long section of dialog, let your eyes wander down the page, and try to get a general impression of the dialog.
   c. When you are finished, turn to Understanding the Plot on page 138 and *write down* answers to as many of the questions as you can.

2. **Scan** (Try to scan in five minutes or less.)
   a. Reread the questions that you were not able to answer from Understanding the Plot on page 138.
   b. Go back to the story and look for only those answers.

3. **Read** the story with care to understand it fully. (There is no time limit.)

"The Lost Phoebe" is about an old man, Henry Reifsneider, who out of sadness and loneliness creates a reality inside his mind that is stronger than the reality outside his mind. Strangely, this **hallucination** is more comforting than frightening, both to the man and to us as readers. The country people in the story are **old-fashioned**: they do not quickly accept change or "new" ways, and they are **astonished,** very greatly surprised, by the change in Henry. But they know and like Henry, and because they are so **fond** of him, their behavior toward him is always **sympathetic;** they always try to help him.

THE LOST PHOEBE

I

Old Henry Reifsneider and his wife Phoebe had lived together for forty-eight years. They had lived three miles from a small town whose population was steadily falling. This part of the country was not as wealthy as it used to be. It wasn't thickly settled, either. Perhaps there was a house every mile or so, with fields in between. Their own house had been built by Henry's grandfather many years ago. A new part had been added to the original log cabin when Henry married Phoebe. The new part was now weather-beaten. Wind whistled through cracks in the boards. Large, lovely trees surrounded the house. But they made it seem a little damp inside.

2   The furniture, like the house, was old. There was a tall cupboard of cherry-wood and a large, old-fashioned bed. The chest of drawers was also high and wide and solidly built. But it had faded, and smelled damp. The carpet that lay under the strong, lasting furniture had been made by Phoebe herself, fifteen years before she died. Now it was worn and faded to a dull gray and pink. The frame that she had made the carpet on was still there. It stood like a dusty, bony skeleton in the east room. All sorts of broken-down

furniture lay around the place. There was a doorless clothes-cupboard. A broken mirror hung in an old cherry-wood frame. It had fallen from a nail and cracked three days before their youngest son, Jerry, died. There was a hatstand whose china knobs had broken off. And an old-fashioned sewing machine.

3   The orchard to the east of the house was full of rotting apple trees. Their twisted branches were covered with greenish-white moss which looked sad and ghostly in the moonlight. Besides the orchard, several low buildings surrounded the house. They had once housed chickens, a horse or two, a cow, and several pigs. The same gray-green moss covered their roofs. They had not been painted for so long that they had turned a grayish-black. In fact, everything on the farm had aged and faded along with Old Henry and his wife Phoebe.

4   They had lived here, these two, since their marriage forty-eight years before. And Henry had lived here as a child. His father and mother had been old when Henry married. They had invited him to bring his wife to the farm. They had all lived together for ten years before his mother and father died. After that Henry and Phoebe were left alone with their four children. But all sorts of things had happened since then. They had had seven children, but three had died. One girl had gone to Kansas. One boy had gone to Sioux Falls and was never even heard from again. Another boy had gone to Washington. The last girl lived five counties away in the same state. She had so many problems of her own, however, that she rarely gave her parents a thought. Their very ordinary home life had never been attractive to the children. So time had drawn them away. Wherever they were, they gave little thought to their father and mother.

5   Old Henry Reifsneider and his wife Phoebe were a loving couple. You perhaps know how it is with such simple people. They fasten themselves like moss on stones, until they and their circumstances are worn away. The larger world has no call to them; or if it does, they don't hear it. The orchard, the fields, the pigpen and the chicken house measure the range of their human activities. When the wheat is ripe, it is harvested. When the corn is full, it is cut. After that comes winter. The grain is taken to market, the wood is cut for the fires. The work is simple: fire-building,

meal-getting, occasional repairing, visiting. There are also changes in the weather—the snow, the rains, and the fair days. Beyond these things, nothing else means very much. All the rest of life is a far-off dream. It shines, far away, like starlight. It sounds as faint as cowbells in the distance.

6   Old Henry and his wife Phoebe were as fond of each other as is possible for two old people who have nothing else in this life to be fond of. He was a thin old man, seventy when she died. He was a strange, moody person with thick, uncombed gray-black hair and beard. He looked at you out of dull, fish-like watery eyes. His clothes, like the clothes of many farmers, were old and ill-fitting. They were too large at the neck. The knees and elbows were stretched and worn. Phoebe was thin and shapeless. Dressed in black, she looked like an umbrella. As time had passed they had only themselves to look after. Their activities had become fewer and fewer. The herd of pigs was reduced to one. The sleepy horse Henry still kept was neither very clean nor well-fed. Almost all the chickens had disappeared. They had been killed by animals or disease. The once-healthy vegetable garden was now only a memory of itself. The flower beds were overgrown. A will had been made which divided the small property equally among the remaining four children. It was so small that it was really of no interest to any of them. Yet Henry and Phoebe lived together in peace and sympathy. Once in a while Old Henry would become moody and annoyed. He would complain that something unimportant had been lost.

7   "Phoebe, where's my corn knife? You never leave my things alone."

8   "Now you be quiet, Henry," his wife would answer in her old cracked voice. "If you don't, I'll leave you. I'll get up and walk out of here one day. Then where would you be? You don't have anybody but me to look after you, so just behave yourself. Your corn knife is in the cupboard where it's always been, unless you put it somewhere else."

9   Old Henry knew his wife would never leave him. But sometimes he wondered what he would do if she died. That was the one leaving he was afraid of. Every night he wound the old clock and went to lock the doors, and it comforted him to know Phoebe was in bed. If he moved in his sleep she would be there to ask him what he wanted.

10   "Now, Henry, do lie still! You're as restless as a chicken."

11   "Well, I can't sleep, Phoebe."

12   "Well, you don't have to roll over so much. You can let *me* sleep." This would usually put him to sleep.

13   If she wanted a pail of water, he complained, but it gave him pleasure to bring it. If she rose first to build the fire, he made sure the wood was cut and placed within easy reach. So they divided this simple world nicely between them.

II

14   In the spring of her sixty-fourth year, Phoebe became sick. Old Henry drove to town and brought back the doctor. But because of her age, her sickness was not curable, and one cold night she died. Henry could have gone to live with his youngest daughter. But it was really too much trouble. He was too weary and used to his home. He wanted to remain near where they had put his Phoebe.

15   His neighbors invited him to stay with them. But he didn't want to. So his friends left him with advice and offers of help. They sent supplies of coffee and bacon and bread. He tried to interest himself in farming to keep himself busy. But it was sad to come into the house in the evening. He could find no shadow of Phoebe, although everything in the house suggested her. At night he read the newspapers that friends had left for him. Or he read his Bible, which he had forgotten about for years. But he could get little comfort from these things. Mostly he sat and wondered where Phoebe had gone, and how soon he would die.

16   He made coffee every morning and fried himself some bacon at night. But he wasn't hungry. His house was empty; its shadows saddened him. So he lived quite unhappily for five long months. And then a change began.

17   It was a moonlight night. The moss-covered orchard shone ghostly silver. As usual, Henry was thinking of Phoebe and the years when they had been young together. And he thought about the children who had gone. The condition of the house was becoming worse. The sheets were not clean, because he made a poor job of the laundry. The roof leaked, and things inside got damp. But he didn't do anything about it. He preferred to walk slowly back and forth, or sit and think.

18   By 12:00 midnight of this particular night, however, he was asleep. He woke up at 2:00. The moon shone in through the living room windows. His coat lying on the back of the chair made a shadow near the table. It looked like Phoebe as she used to sit there. Could it be she—or her ghost? He never used to believe in spirits, and yet . . . He stared at it in the pale light. His old hair seemed to rise up from his head. He sat up, but the figure did not move. He put his thin legs out of the bed. He wondered if this could really be Phoebe. They had often talked about ghosts and spirits. But they had never agreed that such things could be. His wife had never believed that her spirit could return to walk the earth. She had believed in a heaven where good folk would want to stay and not come back. Yet here she was now, bending over the table. She was wearing her black dress. Her face shone pale in the moonlight.

19   "Phoebe," he called, excited from head to toe. "Have you come back?"

20   The figure did not move. He got up and walked uncertainly towards the door, watching it carefully. As he came near, however, the ghost became once more his coat upon the chair.

21   "Well," he said to himself, his mouth open in wonder, "I surely thought I saw her." He ran his hands through his hair while his excitement relaxed. Although it had disappeared, he had the idea that she might return.

22   Another night he looked out of the window toward the chicken house and pigpen. Mist was rising from the damp ground, and he thought he saw Phoebe. She always used to cross from the kitchen door to the pigpen to feed the pigs. And here she was again. He sat up and watched her. He was doubtful because of the first experience. But his body shook with excitement. Perhaps there really were spirits. Phoebe must be worried about his loneliness. She must be thinking about him. He watched her until a breath of wind blew the mist away.

23   A third night, as he was dreaming, she came to his bed.

24   "Poor Henry," she said. "It's too bad." He woke up and thought he saw her move from the bedroom into the living room. He got up, greatly astonished. He was sure that Phoebe was coming back to him. If he thought about her enough, if he showed her how much he needed her, she

would come back. She would tell him what to do. Perhaps she would stay with him most of the time. At least, during the night. That would make him less lonely.

25   For the old or weak, imagination may easily develop into actual hallucination. Eventually this change happened for Henry. Night after night he waited, expecting her return. Once in a strange mood he thought he saw a pale light moving about the room. Another time he saw her walking in the orchard after dark. Then one morning he felt he could not bear his loneliness any longer. He woke up with the knowledge that she was not dead. It is hard to say how he felt so certain. His mind was gone. In its place was the hallucination that he and Phoebe had had a senseless quarrel. He had complained that she had moved his pipe. In the past she had jokingly threatened to leave him if he did not behave himself.

26   "I guess I could find you again," he had always said. But her joking threat had always been the same:

27   "You won't find me if I ever leave you. I guess I can get to some place where you can't find me."

28   When he got up that morning he didn't build the fire or cut the bread as usual. He began to think where he should look for her. He put on his soft hat and took his walking-stick from behind the door. He started out energetically to look for her among his neighbors. His old shoes scratched loudly in the dust. His gray hair, now grown rather long, hung down below his hat. His hands and face were pale.

29   "Why, hello, Henry! Where are you going this morning?" inquired Farmer Dodge.

30   "You haven't seen Phoebe, have you?"

31   "Phoebe who?" asked Farmer Dodge. He didn't connect the name with Henry's dead wife.

32   "Why, my wife, Phoebe, of course. Who do you suppose I mean?"

33   "Oh, come on, Henry! You aren't joking, are you? It can't be your wife you're talking about. She's dead."

34   "Dead? Not Phoebe! She left me early this morning while I was sleeping. We had a little quarrel last night, and I guess that's the reason. But I guess I can find her. She's gone over to Matilda Race's, that's where she's gone."

35   He started quickly up the road. The astonished Dodge stared after him. "Well!" he said to himself. "He's gone

crazy. That poor old man has lived down there alone until he's gone completely out of his mind. I'll have to inform the police."

36   "Why, Mr. Reifsneider," cried old Matilda Race as Henry knocked on her door. "What brings you here this morning?"

37   "Is Phoebe here?" he demanded eagerly.

38   "Phoebe who? What Phoebe?" replied Mrs. Race, curious.

39   "Why, my Phoebe, of course, my wife Phoebe. Who do you suppose? Isn't she here now?"

40   "Why, you poor man!" cried Mrs. Race. "You've lost your mind. You come right in and sit down. I'll get you a cup of coffee. Of course your wife isn't here. But you come in and sit down. I'll find her for you after a while. I know where she is."

41   The old farmer's eyes softened at her sympathy.

42   "We had a quarrel last night and she left me," Henry offered.

43   "Oh, my!" Mrs. Race sighed to herself. There was no one there to share her astonishment. "The poor man! Now somebody's just got to look after him. He can't be allowed to run around the country this way looking for his dead wife. It's terrible."

44   She boiled him a pot of coffee and brought in some new-baked bread and fresh butter. She put on a couple of eggs to boil, lying as she spoke:

45   "Now, you stay right there, Henry, until Jake comes in. I'll send him to look for Phoebe. I think she must be over at Sumnerton with some of her friends. Anyhow, we'll find out. Now you just drink this coffee and eat this bread. You must be tired. You've had a long walk this morning." Her idea was to wait for her husband, Jake, and perhaps have him call the police.

46   Henry ate, but his mind was on his wife. Since she was not here, perhaps she was visiting the Murrays—miles away in another direction. He decided that he would not wait for Jake Race. He would search for his wife himself.

47   "Well, I'll be going," he said, getting up and looking strangely about him. "I guess she didn't come here after all. She went over to the Murrays', I guess." And he marched out, ignoring Matilda Race's cries of worry.

48   Two hours later his dusty, eager figure appeared in the Murrays' doorway. He had walked five miles and it was noon. The Murrays, a husband and wife of sixty, listened to him with astonishment. They also realized that he was mad. They invited him to stay to dinner. They intended to call the police later, to see what could be done. But Henry did not stay long. His need for Phoebe pulled him off to another distant farmhouse. So it went for that day and the next and the next. And the circle of his questioning grew wider and wider.

49   And although Henry came to many doors, and the police were informed, it was decided not to send him to the county hospital. The condition of mad patients in this hospital was horrifying. It was found that Henry returned peaceably to his lonely home at night to see if his wife had returned. Who would lock up a thin, eager, old man with gray hair and a kindly, innocent, inquiring manner? His neighbors had known him as a kindly, dependable man. He could do no harm. Many people gave him food and old clothes—at least at first. His figure became a common sight, and the answer, "Why no, Henry, I haven't seen her," or, "No, Henry, she hasn't been here today," became more customary.

III

50   For several years afterward he was an odd figure in the sun and rain, on dusty roads and muddy ones. The longer he walked in this manner, the deeper his strange hallucination became. He found it harder and harder to return from his more and more distant searches. Finally he began to take a few eating utensils with him so he would not have to return home at night. In an old coffeepot he put a small tin cup. He took a knife, fork, and spoon, and salt and pepper. He tied a tin plate to the pot. It was no trouble for him to get the little food he needed. And with a strange, almost religious manner, he didn't hesitate to ask for that much. Slowly his hair became longer and longer. His black hat became an earthen brown, and his clothes worn and dusty.

51   For three years he walked with only his clothes, his stick, and his utensils. No one knew how far he went, or how he lived through the storms and cold. They did not see him find shelter in piles of grass or by the sides of cattle. The warm bodies of the cows protected him from cold, and their

dull minds did not oppose his presence. Overhanging rocks and trees kept him from the rain.

52   The progress of such hallucinations is strange. He had asked for Phoebe at people's doors and got no answer. Finally he decided that she was not in any of the houses. But she might be within reach of his voice. So he began to call sad, occasional cries. "O-o-o Phoebe! O-o-o Phoebe!" waked the quiet countryside and echoed through the hills. It had a sad, mad ring. Many farmers recognized it from far away and said, "There goes old Reifsneider."

53   Sometimes when he reached a crossroad, he couldn't decide which way to go. He developed another hallucination to help him. He believed Phoebe's spirit or some power of the air or wind or nature would tell him where to go. He would stand at the crossroad and close his eyes. He would turn around three times and call "O-o-o Phoebe" twice. Then he would throw his walking stick straight before him. This would surely tell him which way to go. Phoebe or some magic power would direct the stick. He would then follow the direction the stick pointed, even when it led him back the way he had come. And the hallucination that he would surely find her remained. There were hours when his feet were sore and his legs tired. There were times when he would stop in the heat to wipe his forehead, or in the cold to beat his arms. Sometimes, after throwing his stick and finding it pointing to where he had just come from, he would shake his head wearily and philosophically. He would consider for a moment the confusion and disappointment of life, and his own strange fate. Then he would start energetically off again. His strange figure finally became known in the farthest corners of three or four counties. Old Reifsneider was a sad character. His fame was wide.

54   About four miles from the little town called Watersville there was a place called Red Cliff. This cliff was a steep wall of red sandstone, perhaps a hundred feet high. It rose above the fruitful corn fields and orchards that lay beneath. Trees grew thickly along the top of the cliff. In fair weather it was old Reifsneider's habit to spend the night here. He would fry his bacon or boil his eggs at the foot of some tree. Then he would lie down.

55   He almost always woke at 2:00 in the morning. Occasionally he would walk at night. More often he would

sit up and watch the darkness or the stars, wondering. Sometimes in the strangeness of his mind he imagined he saw his lost wife moving among the trees. Then he would get up to follow. He would take his utensils on a string, and his stick. When she tried to escape him he would run after her, begging. When she disappeared he would feel disappointed. He was saddened at the almost impossible difficulties of his search.

56   One night in the seventh year of his search he came to the top of Red Cliff. It was spring, like the spring when Phoebe had died. He had walked many many miles with his utensils, following his walking stick. It was after 10:00 at night. He was very tired. Long walking and little eating had left him only a shadow of his former self. He had little strength. Only his hallucination kept him going. He had eaten hardly anything that day. Now, exhausted, he lay down in the dark to rest and possibly sleep.

57   He felt the presence of his wife strongly. It would not be long now until he should see her, talk to her, he told himself. He fell asleep, after a time, his head on his knees. At midnight the moon began to rise. At 2:00 in the morning, his wakeful hour, it was a large silver ball. He opened his eyes. The moonlight made silvery patterns at his feet. The forest was full of strange light and silvery, shadowy forms. What was it that moved among the trees— a pale, shining, ghostly figure? Moonlight and shadow gave it a strange form and a stranger reality. Was it truly his lost Phoebe? It came near him. He imagined he could see her eyes. Not as she was when he last saw her in the black dress and shawl. Now she was a strangely younger Phoebe. She was the one whom he had known years before as a girl. Old Reifsneider got up. He had been expecting and dreaming of this hour all these years. Now he saw the pale light dancing before him. He looked at it questioningly, one hand on his gray hair.

58   For the first time in many years he suddenly remembered the full beauty of the girlish form. He saw her pleasing, sympathetic smile, her brown hair. He remembered the blue ribbon she had once worn about her waist. He saw her light and happy movements. He forgot his pots and pans and followed her. She moved before him and it seemed that she waved to him with a young and playful hand.

59   "Oh, Phoebe! Phoebe!" he called. "Have you really come? Have you really answered me?" On and on he hurried until he was almost running. He brushed his arms against the trees. He struck his hands and face against small branches. His hat was gone, his breath was gone, his mind quite gone when he came to the edge of the cliff. Down below he saw her among the silver apple trees now blooming in the spring.

60   "Oh, Phoebe!" he called. "Oh, Phoebe! Oh no, don't leave me!" He felt the pull of the world where love was young and Phoebe waited. "Oh, wait, Phoebe!" he cried, and jumped.

61   Some farm boys found his utensils under the tree where he had left them. Later, at the foot of the cliff, they found his body. He was pale and broken, but full of happiness. A smile of peace curved his lips. His old hat was discovered under a tree. No one of all the simple population knew how eagerly and happily he had finally found his lost Phoebe.

AFTER YOU READ THE STORY

A. Understanding the Plot

Answer the following questions with complete sentences.

1. How long had Henry and Phoebe been married?
2. Had their marriage been a happy or an unhappy one?
3. What was their relationship to their neighbors? To their children? To the rest of the world generally?
4. What does Henry imagine he sees, after Phoebe dies?
5. Why does Henry leave home? How would you describe his behavior as he walks all over the countryside?
6. How long does he continue to search for Phoebe?
7. What happens to Henry on the top of Red Cliff?

B. Close Reading

Part I (pages 126–130)
In Part I, Dreiser gives us important details about Henry Reifsneider's life to help us understand his situation exactly. Do you remember these details? If not, can you find them?

1. When was the "new part" of Henry's house added to the original log cabin? What did this "new part" look like now? (paragraph 1)
2. Eight pieces of furniture are mentioned. What are they? Which two pieces give us information about two members of Henry's family? (paragraph 2)
3. What covered both the roof of the buildings and the trees of the orchard? (paragraph 3)
4. Which sentence in paragraph 3 summarizes the condition of Old Henry's farm?
5. Henry and Phoebe had seven children. What became of each of these children? (paragraph 4)
6. What activities filled the lives of Henry and Phoebe? List at least six. (paragraph 5)

Part II (pages 130–134)
In Part II, Dreiser is careful to show us that, following Phoebe's death, Henry develops his hallucination not immediately, but slowly over many months. In the following sentences, choose the phrase or phrases that best show how Henry's madness grew. Paragraph numbers are given to help you find the correct answer.

1. In the first five months following Phoebe's death, (paragraphs 14–17)
   a. Henry decided not to live with his youngest daughter.
   b. Henry tried to live his normal life, eating and farming and reading.
   c. the condition of Henry's house slowly worsened.
   d. All the above are correct.

2. One night after midnight, the shadow of Henry's coat on a chair (paragraphs 18–21)
   a. looked to Henry like Phoebe in her black dress.
   b. made Henry sure he was seeing Phoebe's ghost, or spirit.
   c. gave Henry the idea that Phoebe might return.
   d. Two of the above are correct.

3. On a second night, when Henry thought he saw Phoebe in the mist near the pigpen, (paragraph 22)
   a. he realized that she was crossing from the kitchen door to feed the pigs.
   b. he was doubtful, yet his body shook with excitement.

    c. it made him *fear* that somehow Phoebe was trying to harm him.

    d. All the above are correct.

4. Henry became certain that Phoebe was not dead (paragraphs 23–27)

    a. when she came to his bed and spoke to him.

    b. mainly because he could not bear his loneliness any longer.

    c. because in the past he and Phoebe had had senseless quarrels.

    d. Two of the above are correct.

5. When Henry went to his neighbors looking for Phoebe, (paragraphs 28–49)

    a. they understood that he had lost his mind.

    b. they were astonished by him but kind to him.

    c. some later called the police, but in the end no one stopped Henry's search because he was peaceful.

    d. All the above are correct.

Part III (pages 134–138)

Below are phrases and statements from Part III. Ask questions for which each phrase or statement is the answer. There may be more than one possible question for each phrase or statement.

Example: On dusty roads and muddy ones. (paragraph 50)

> **Where did Henry walk on his travels?**
>
> or
>
> **What kinds of roads did Henry walk on?**

1. In piles of grass or by the sides of cattle. (paragraph 51)
2. "O-o-o Phoebe! O-o-o Phoebe!" (paragraph 52)
3. This would surely tell him which way to go. (paragraph 53)
4. Red Cliff. (paragraph 54)
5. These had left him only a shadow of his former self. (paragraph 56)
6. Young, beautiful, and girlish. (paragraphs 57, 58)
7. His hat, his breath, and his mind. (paragraph 59)

8. Down below him, among the silver apple trees. (paragraph 59)
9. The pull of the world where love was young and Phoebe waited. (paragraph 60)
10. No one. (paragraph 61)

C. Vocabulary Practice

In the following quotations from the story, one word is underlined. After considering the word in its context, and without looking it up in the dictionary, choose the best definition for the word. Be prepared to explain why you chose it.

Example: *Large, lovely trees surrounded the house. But they made it seem a little <u>damp</u> inside.* (paragraph 1)

    a. pretty **b.** cool and wet **c.** very unpleasant

The best definition is "cool and wet." The "lovely trees" would shade out the sun and possibly cause wetness. "Pretty" is not a good definition because the word *but* that begins the sentence puts *damp* in contrast to "lovely" (pretty). "Very unpleasant" is not a good definition because the phrase *a little* does not suggest something "*very* unpleasant."

1. *Once in a while Old Henry would become <u>moody</u> and annoyed. He would complain that something important had been lost.* (paragraph 6)

    a. depressed **b.** philosophical **c.** very serious

2.   *"Why, you poor man!" cried Mrs. Race. "You've lost your mind. You come right in and sit down. I'll get you a cup of coffee . . . "*
   The old farmer's eyes softened at her <u>sympathy</u>. (paragraphs 40–41)

    a. mixed feelings **b.** shared feelings **c.** feelings of shock

3. *Who would lock up a thin, eager, old man with gray hair and a kindly, innocent, inquiring manner? His neighbors had known him as a kindly, dependable man. He could do no <u>harm</u>.* (paragraph 49)

    a. any action **b.** a good action **c.** a bad action

4. *Finally he began to take a few eating <u>utensils</u> with him. . . . In an old coffee pot he put a small tin cup. He took a knife, fork, and spoon, and salt and pepper.* (paragraph 50)

   a. types of food   **b.** small tools   **c.** coffee-making things

5. *This <u>cliff</u> was a steep wall of red sandstone, perhaps a hundred feet high. It rose above the fruitful corn fields and orchards that lay beneath.* (paragraph 54)

   a. a field high in the air   **b.** a high wall to protect fields
   c. the rock face of a hill that drops straight down

D. Word Forms

Noun	Verb	Adjective	Adverb
astonishment	astonish	astonishing	astonishingly
hallucination	hallucinate	hallucinatory	
madness	madden	maddening	maddeningly
quarrel	quarrel	quarrelsome	quarrelsomely
sadness	sadden	sad	sadly
sympathy	sympathize	sympathetic	sympathetically
wonderment	wonder	wondering	wonderingly

Rewrite the following sentences, keeping their basic meaning but using a different form of the italicized word. Use the form called for in the parentheses, and make other changes to the original sentence as necessary.

Example: Henry felt the presence of his wife strongly; yet she remained *maddeningly* out of sight, beyond his reach.

(adjective) <u>Henry felt the presence of his wife strongly; yet she</u>
<u>remained out of sight, beyond his reach, and this was maddening</u>
<u>to him.</u>

1. To the *astonishment* of his neighbors, Henry looked like a
   madman; yet they treated him with kindness.

   (adjective) _____

   _____

2. Mrs. Race felt *sad* because of Henry's condition, but she made him breakfast with an almost cheerful manner.

(verb) _____

_____

3. Phoebe's appearing to be alive was *hallucinatory*, a product only of Henry's mind.

(noun) _____

_____

4. As a couple, Henry and Phoebe did not really *quarrel*; if Phoebe threatened to leave Henry, she did it only jokingly.

(adjective) _____

_____

5. Having heard Henry's story about looking for Phoebe, Farmer Dodge could only stare in *wonderment* after the man when he walked down the road.

(adverb) _____

_____

6. At the end of the story, Henry remembers Phoebe's pleasing, *sympathetic* smile.

(adverb) _____

_____

E. Language Activity: Figurative Language

If a story's sense of reality comes from its details, the atmosphere of a story comes from the writer's use of language. *Figurative language* is the use of words to create meaningful pictures in the reader's mind. Examples of, and questions about, Dreiser's use of figurative language follow. Working with a partner, answer the questions below, and add your own examples of figurative language as requested.

1. The frame for making carpets stood "like a dusty, bony skeleton in the east room." (paragraph 2) What does this phrase tell us about the frame? about the general appearance of the east room? Picture a piece of furniture in your own room, apartment, or house. What can you compare it to (what is it *like*?) that will help others see it and get a sense of the whole room?

2. The life of the world outside the farm is, to the Reifsneiders, like a "far-off dream. It shines, far away, like starlight. It sounds as faint as cowbells in the distance." (paragraph 5) In trying to describe this outside world, Dreiser tells us how it feels (like a dream), what it looks like (far-away starlight), and what it sounds like (faint as distant cowbells). With these phrases in mind, tell in your own words what the "outside" world means to the Reifsneiders. Then think of a place, town, city, or country you know, and say what it feels like, looks like, and sounds like.

3. What does Phoebe mean when she says that Henry is "as restless as a chicken"? (paragraph 10) Then use the same kind of phrase—*as* (adjective) *as a* (kind of animal)—to describe your best friend, worst enemy, or someone in your family.

F. Discussion: Respect for Old Henry

In some ways, Henry Reifsneider is a comic character. Dreiser, in fact, is careful not to hide the funny side of Old Henry's hallucination. In the scenes with Farmer Dodge and Matilda Race, or when he turns around three times and throws his stick, we are likely to be amused as well as sympathetic. In the end, however, our sympathy for Henry is greater than our amusement. We grow to respect and even admire him because, in his search for his lost Phoebe, he shows certain qualities of character that we admire whenever we find them.

Reread the following passage from the story (paragraph 53):

> There were hours when his feet were sore and his legs tired. There were times when he would stop in the heat to wipe his forehead, or in the cold to beat his arms. Sometimes, after throwing his stick and finding it pointing to where he had just come from, he would shake his head wearily and philosophically. He would consider

for a moment the confusion and disappointment of life,
and his own strange fate. Then he would start
energetically off again. His strange figure finally became
known in the farthest corners of three or four counties.

Working with a partner or a small group of other students, discuss the following questions. Be prepared to report your answers and opinions to the rest of the class.

- What in the above passage wins our admiration for Henry? What are the strengths he shows us in his madness?
- What other admirable human qualities in Henry can you remember from other scenes in the story? (Think of the final scene among the trees on Red Cliff, for example.)
- Are these qualities worth less in Henry than they would be in a person who was not mad? Are they worth more?
- In short: Henry has lost his mind. The quality of reason is gone. What qualities remain?

G. Writing: An Analysis of Old Henry's Character

Working again with a partner, plan a three-paragraph composition on the character of Old Henry. After completing Discussion: Respect for Old Henry, decide how to organize the ideas you have talked about. Then write your compositions separately, show them to each other, and discuss and correct them. Your composition should answer the three general questions below, and your answers should be supported by events and/or quotations from Dreiser's story.

Paragraph 1: What were the basic elements of Henry's character when Phoebe was alive?
Paragraph 2: As Henry develops his hallucination about Phoebe after her death, what elements of his character deepen, and what new elements are added?
Paragraph 3: Which elements of Henry's character have left him just before the end, and which elements remain?

When you have finished these three paragraphs, write a short beginning paragraph that introduces the subject to your reader and a short final paragraph that summarizes your views about Henry's character.

ANSWER KEY

Note: Generally, no answers are given to questions that ask for the reader's opinion. But sample answers are given for exercises in which the student is asked to use his or her own words. Samples are also given for the more controlled writing exercises, but not for those that encourage freedom of expression.

1. THE ROMANCE OF A BUSY BROKER

BEFORE YOU READ THE STORY

A. About the Author

He had many different jobs. I would expect the characters in his stories to be ordinary people.

D. Scanning for Information

1. North Carolina
2. O. Henry
3. fifteen
4. a drugstore, a business office, a building designer's office, a bank
5. in prison
6. a book of adventure stories
7. short stories with surprise endings
8. ordinary people of New York City

AFTER YOU READ THE STORY

A. Understanding the Plot

1. Maxwell is a stockbroker.
2. A man named Pitcher and a woman named Miss Leslie work with Maxwell. Pitcher is an assistant; Miss Leslie is Maxwell's secretary. In the picture, Pitcher is sitting and writing at his desk. Maxwell is standing and studying ticker tape.
3. Pitcher is interested because this morning Maxwell arrived together with his secretary and because at first the secretary did not go to her own desk, but stayed in the outside office.

4. Yesterday, Pitcher called the secretarial school because Maxwell wanted to hire a new secretary.
5. He asks her to be his wife.
6. She is surprised because they were married the night before.

B. Close Reading

1. F. Pitcher was a quiet man, and he didn't usually let his face show his feelings.
2. T.
3. F. She seemed very happy, and she always dressed simply but beautifully.
4. T.
5. T.
6. F. The office was very busy and full of action.
7. F. He told Pitcher that the job was Miss Leslie's.

C. Vocabulary Practice

1. busier
2. stocks
3. faster
4. harder
5. feelings
6. quieted
7. flowers
8. office
9. smiled
10. hurry
11. marry
12. cry
13. tears
14. business
15. married
16. church

D. Word Forms

1. surprised, surprise, surprise
2. interested, interest, interested
3. crowded, crowd, crowded
4. dress, dressed, dress
5. changed, change, changed

E. Language Activity: The New York Stock Exchange

1. Toyota, Polaroid
2. Boeing (upward 2.29), Radio Shack (downward 3.38)
3. Toyota, Polaroid
4. Answers can vary, but, for example: If you want to buy at a price that is low compared to previous highs, in the hope that the price will rise again: Polaroid. If you want good value compared to last year's prices: Boeing or General Electric. If you're in love with the entertainment industry: Disney. If you want a company that seems to be coming back well from last year's low: Toyota. Etc.

G. Writing: Controlled Composition

Pitcher worked in the office of Harvey Maxwell, a stockbroker. Usually he was a quiet man. But this morning he acted surprised and very interested. Maxwell had arrived together with his secretary, Miss Leslie. He usually arrived alone. After Maxwell said, "Good morning," he ran to his desk. Miss Leslie asked Pitcher if Maxwell had asked him to hire another secretary yesterday. Then she went to her desk to work until the new secretary came. As the morning passed, the office seemed very busy, and Maxwell acted like a machine of many moving parts. Then another woman came into the office. She had come for the secretarial job. Maxwell said nothing to her, but yelled at Pitcher that the job was Miss Leslie's. The woman felt very angry, and she left. Later, near lunchtime, everything quieted down. Maxwell suddenly smelled flowers. The smell made Maxwell think of Miss Leslie. He decided to ask her to marry him. When he went to Miss Leslie's office, he said, "Will you be my wife?" At first, she seemed surprised, and she cried. Later, she understood that the business had made him forget. He had forgotten that they were married last night in the little church around the corner.

2. THE INGRATE

BEFORE YOU READ THE STORY

A. About the Author

Dunbar's father was an escaped slave, like Josh in the story. During his lifetime, Dunbar was known for his poetry more than his novels and stories.

D. Scanning

1. a person who shows no gratitude, who gives no thanks for help or kindness shown to him or her
2. Josh and Mr. Leckler
3. a religious group

AFTER YOU READ THE STORY

A. Understanding the Plot

1. Josh worked as a plasterer on Mr. Leckler's plantation.
2. Leckler let Josh work on other plantations because the other owners paid him for Josh's work.
3. Josh was saving money to buy his freedom.
4. Josh escaped by writing himself a pass that allowed him to get on a train, and then by hiding in a bag among bags of corn and potatoes. He went to Canada.
5. The Civil War began.
6. Josh was made an officer. Mr. Leckler learned about it when he saw Josh's name on a list of black soldiers.

B. Close Reading

Part I

1. He says that he is troubled by a matter of principle.
2. He says he is angry because Mr. Eckley is cheating Josh.
3. He says he will teach Josh to read and do numbers so that Josh can defend himself against being cheated.
4. His real reason is that he keeps nine-tenths of what Josh earns, so Mr. Eckley is cheating him more than he is cheating Josh.
5. He says that in this way Josh will be able to buy his freedom.
6. Mr. Leckler plans to raise the price of freedom when Josh gets close to saving $2,000.

Parts II and III

1. c
2. b
3. a
4. c
5. b

C. Vocabulary Practice

1. dishonest, honest
2. generous, ungenerous
3. troubled, untroubled
4. obedient, disobedient
5. grateful, ungrateful

D. Word Forms

1. advised, advice
2. earned, earnings
3. taught, teaching
4. building, built
5. obedience, obeyed
6. cheating, cheated

G. Writing: A Speech to the Abolitionists (sample speech)

Ladies and Gentlemen, Brothers and Sisters: My name is Joshua
Leckler, and I have escaped from slavery. I was a slave all my life,
until last year. The man who called himself my master was
named James Leckler. I worked as a plasterer on his plantation. I
did the same work for other slave owners who paid Mr. Leckler
for my work. I was allowed to keep one-tenth of this money for
myself. I planned to buy my freedom after I had saved $2,000.
Mr. Leckler decided to help me learn to read and do numbers so
that other slave owners would not cheat me, which meant he
would make more money himself. I thought this education might
help me to become a free man.

I escaped from Mr. Leckler by writing a pass for myself to
get on a train north. Later, I hid in a bag on a wagon with other
bags of corn and potatoes. Abolitionists, Quakers, and other
freed slaves helped me escape. It felt strange and wonderful to be
free. I was a man like other men. I was paid for what my work
was worth. I have come to Boston now to sign up for the
northern army. At this moment in my life, I am most worried
about the lives of my brothers and sisters in the South who are
still slaves. I am grateful for my own freedom, and I promise you
this: I will not stop fighting for freedom until every black man,
woman, and child is free. Thank you.

3. HOW I WENT TO THE MINES

BEFORE YOU READ THE STORY

A. About the Author

He is best known for his "local color" stories. He moved to
Europe because his money and fame did not last long; he

worked in Europe as a businessman and U.S. consul. He lived
outside the United States for twenty-five years, until his death in
England in 1902.

D. Skimming to Get an Impression

1. California
2. schoolmaster
3. to the gold mines, because his school closed and San
   Francisco was far away
4. in the woods
5. disappointed

AFTER YOU READ THE STORY

A. Understanding the Plot

1. He is a schoolmaster. He leaves this job because his school
   closes (because two families and about twelve children move
   away, and there is not enough money to keep the school
   open).
2. He decides to become a gold digger. He hopes to find a
   miner named Jim whom he met once in San Francisco.
3. He travels on foot because he doesn't have enough money to
   travel by horse and wagon.
4. Two men start a gunfight, with the young man caught in the
   middle of it.
5. He discovers that Jim has left his partners and returned to
   San Francisco. The three remaining partners offer him Jim's
   place in the partnership.
6. He finds small pieces of gold not worth much and one
   nugget worth about twelve dollars. He and his partners
   never find another nugget, but they usually find enough gold
   to pay for their daily food.

B. Close Reading

Part I
1. He states that most of the cost was carried by a few families.
2. We expect the high school teacher to be at least four to six
   years older than his oldest students, but the young man had
   a student who was a year older than he was.

3. We might expect a student to give his or her teacher a pen or a book or another small gift, but the young man's student gave him a huge piece of gingerbread. It became his only food on his journey to the mines.
4. We might expect him to spend it on his travel or to save it for his arrival at the mines, but instead he spent $5 (70%) of it on a revolver.

Part II
1. a
2. c
3. b
4. c

Part III
The following sentences should be checked:

1. The cabin's walls had holes in them. The furniture included three boxes to sit on or eat from.
2. showed confidence even in strangers; could dig for gold on any land that someone else had not claimed; worked hard, but without much result; believed that it was not a bad thing to lack gold-mining experience.
3. The miners used their tools in the following order: pick, shovel, pan.

C. Vocabulary Practice: Understanding Words in Context

1. The young man shows that he is extravagant by spending a lot of money on fine shirts when he has only a little money.
2. The young man had blistered feet because he had walked for many miles in rough or wild country in shoes that were made for town (or the classroom).
3. The young man limped because his feet hurt him so much, especially after he put his terrible shoes back on.
4. The young man would feel ashamed to ask his question unless he bought a drink, and this was because the barkeeper looked so important to him.
5. The miners showed their confidence by telling the young man he could be a partner, when they knew almost nothing about him.

D. Word Forms

1. employed
2. embarrassed
3. disappointed
4. recognition
5. encouraged
6. confident

4. PAUL'S CASE

BEFORE YOU READ THE STORY

A. About the Author

Pioneers and artists (painters, writers, and theater people). Both kinds explored unsettled areas—of thought and feeling for the artists, of land for the pioneers.

D. Scanning for Context

(sample definitions)

1. An *usher* shows us to our seats at a concert, play, or movie.
2. A *uniform* is the special clothing worn by people who belong to the same group or profession. (Soldiers wear uniforms, and sometimes so do ushers.)
3. An *aisle* is the open space we walk down on our way to our seats in a theater (or church).

AFTER YOU READ THE STORY

A. Understanding the Plot

1. He had to meet with his teachers; he had been suspended for a week, and he had to explain his bad behavior to them and say he wanted to come back to school.
2. They are angry because Paul is offensive in class and has a contemptuous attitude toward them.
3. Paul goes to the concert hall (Carnegie Hall), where he is an usher.

4. Paul hates Cordelia Street and loves the world of the theater and concert hall.
5. He is taken out of school because he does not improve, and he is put to work as a clerk in a business, Denny & Carson.
6. He runs away to New York City and lives the life he has always dreamed of living.
7. He pays for the trip by stealing money from Denny & Carson.
8. After Paul reads the newspaper that tells what he has done, he takes a taxi into the country, walks along the train tracks, and finally jumps in front of a train and is killed.

B. Close Reading

Part I
1. He had behaved badly in school.
2. No, he answered politely that he wanted to come back. This was a lie, but he needed to lie to solve his problems.
3. He had a red carnation in his coat.
4. His teachers left the meeting angry and unhappy.
5. His job excited him. It made him feel like the host of a great party.
6. He hated to give up the excitement and color of the concert; that is why he felt depressed.
7. The hotel's elegance was nothing like his ordinary life at home and at school. He imagines an elegant place, with delicious platters of food and green wine bottles in shining ice buckets.

Part II
1. The houses all looked alike. It was a neighborhood of large families. The children went to Sunday school; they liked geometry; they were all alike. His room had ugly yellow wallpaper. The bathroom was cold and had a dirty tub and broken mirror. His father had hairy legs sticking out from under his nightshirt.
2. He spent the night in the basement, sitting near the furnace, afraid of rats, thinking dark, imaginative thoughts. He spent the night that way because he hadn't wanted to go in the house and explain his lateness to his angry father.
3. The men were small businessmen and clerks. They gave advice about business and the cost of things, and they talked

about the rich and powerful men who were their bosses. The women talked about sewing and children.

4. He shook a few drops of cologne over his fingers.
5. He was put to work as a clerk. He was not allowed to be an usher. He was not allowed to enter the theater. Charley Edwards promised not to see him again.

Part III
1. He orders flowers because they are "the one thing that was missing." They add softness to the air, a nice smell, like springtime. They contrast with the snow "falling wildly" outside.
2. Outside, snow is falling against the shop windows, which inside are full of spring flowers.
3. He understands that they, like him, had only "one bright breath of life." When he buries one of the carnations in the snow, he is burying the most important part of himself—a part that can no longer live.

C. Vocabulary Practice

(sample answers)

1. These thoughts are of rats and of his father killing him by accident, or maybe not by accident.
2. He is excited by the artificial world of the theater because it is so different from the everyday, ugly, boring world of home and school.
3. He is surprised he has the courage to do this, because he had always been afraid of things ever since he was a little boy.
4. The hotel manager was not suspicious of Paul because Paul was quiet and did not draw attention to himself.
5. When Paul reads in the newspaper that his father is coming to New York to look for him, he feels terrible because it means he will probably have to return to Cordelia Street, to his ugly room and ugly life—something worse than jail.
6. As he throws himself in front of the train, Paul feels regret for the things he hasn't done in his life.

D. Word Forms

1. a. offense   b. offensive   c. offend
2. a. pressure   b. pressured   c. pressured
3. a. depress   b. depression   c. depressed
4. a. imaginative   b. imagination   c. imagined

5. A JURY OF HER PEERS

BEFORE YOU READ THE STORY

A. About the Author

Trifles is a play. "A Jury of Her Peers" is a short story.

D. Skimming to Get an Impression

1. cold
2. country
3. both
4. serious

AFTER YOU READ THE STORY

A. Understanding the Plot

1. She was making bread. The sheriff wanted her to come because his wife was nervous and wanted the company of another woman.
2. He found Mrs. Wright acting strangely and Mr. Wright dead, with a rope around his neck.
3. They say that her housekeeping is not very good.
4. They need to find a clue to Mrs. Wright's motive for killing her husband—something to show anger or sudden feeling.
5. The quilt block was badly sewn. Martha begins to replace bad sewing with good.
6. In the box was a dead bird with a broken neck.
7. Martha Hale puts the box in her pocket so that the men will not see it.

B. Close Reading

Part I

1. f
2. c
3. b
4. a
5. d
6. g
7. e
8. c
9. b
10. a

Part II

1. He doesn't think kitchen things are very important.
2. He thinks her interest in her jars of fruit is strange and silly. He implies that women often worry about unimportant things.

3. He implies that women's concerns are not to be taken seriously.
4. He implies that the "ladies" are nice but that their interests are not as important as men's interests. The women's behavior tells us that they feel insulted and angry at his implication.
5. She implies that men are messy and that they don't care about the work they make for women with their messiness.

Part III
1. Clues that Mrs. Wright had interrupted herself, or had been interrupted, in the middle of work: messy pans under the sink, half-empty bag of sugar, half-cleaned table (paragraphs 58–61)
2. Clues that her life was very hard:
   - poor clothes, (paragraphs 63, 64)
   - broken stove, (paragraphs 73, 74)
   - no running water, (paragraph 74)
   - the messily sewn quilt block, showing nervousness (paragraph 79)
   - the bird cage with the broken door, showing someone had broken into the cage with anger or violence (paragraphs 87–90)
   - the dead bird with its broken neck (paragraphs 98, 99) The women believe that John Wright killed the one beautiful or pleasant thing left in his wife's life—the bird.

C. Vocabulary Practice

1. c   2. e   3. d   4. b   5. a

(sample sentences)

6. *county* Mr. Peters, the sheriff, had responsibility for the whole county, which included two towns and some areas in the country that belonged to no towns at all.
7. *attorney* After Mrs. Wright went to jail, she decided she needed an attorney to get her out of jail.
8. *clue* The bird with the broken neck was a clue to Mrs. Wright's reason for murdering her husband.
9. *murder* The sheriff wants to prove that Mrs. Wright is guilty of murder. He needs to know why she would kill her husband.
10. *motive* We don't know what motive Mr. Wright had for breaking the bird's neck. We can guess what motive Mrs. Wright had for strangling her husband.

D. Word Forms

1. a. peaceful   b. peacefully   c. peace
2. a. nervous   b. nervousness   c. nervously
3. a. duty   b. dutiful   c. dutifully
4. a. messy   b. mess   c. messily

G. Writing: A Dialog

(sample continuation of the dialog)

Mrs. Hale: It was the bird, Mrs. Wright. The bird with the broken neck.

Mrs. Wright: Oh, dear. Yes. The bird . . .

Mrs. Peters: *He* killed it, didn't he, Mrs. Wright?

Mrs. Wright: Yes. Yes, he did. The bird was singing, you see, and he just came into the kitchen where I was working, and broke open the cage, and took the bird, and . . . oh, dear, it was so terrible . . .

Mrs. Hale: We told no one about that bird, Mrs. Wright. And neither should you. It would hurt you.

Mrs. Wright: Hurt me?

Mrs. Peters: You see, my husband would consider it proof of your motive for . . . for . . . *you* know . . .

Mrs. Wright: Yes. I do know. But I don't want you to get into trouble.

Mrs. Hale: Actually, Mrs. Peters did nothing. She doesn't know where the dead bird is. Do you, Mrs. Peters?

Mrs. Peters: Well, no, I don't . . .

Mrs. Hale: All right, then. And I'm saying nothing. What the men don't know won't hurt anyone. Not now. Not anymore.

6. THE WHALE HUNT

BEFORE YOU READ THE STORY

A. About the Author

He used his experiences at sea. The *Pequod* was a whaling ship, and Moby Dick was a huge white sperm whale in Melville's novel *Moby Dick*.

D. Scanning for Numbers

1. 1831
2. 1838
3. twenty-two
4. 1866
5. seventy-two

AFTER YOU READ THE STORY

A. Understanding the Plot

1. It is hot and still, and storm clouds are overhead. The men are lying lazily on deck or staring from the masts out to sea.
2. He calls, "There she blows!" because he has seen a school of sperm whales.
3. The men lower the boats in which they will chase the whales, and they jump down into them from the deck of the *Pequod*.
4. Ishmael's boat gets turned over by the whale. The men are thrown into the sea. The whale escapes.
5. The *Pequod* almost crashes into it coming out of the fog. At the end of the story, the men are safely on the deck of the *Pequod*.

B. Close Reading

Part I
1. d 2. e 3. a 4. c 5. b

Part II
1. Starbuck 3. Flask 5. Flask 7. Stubb
2. Flask 4. Stubb 6. Ahab

Part III
a. 8   f. 6
b. 2   g. 3
c. 4   h. 10
d. 9   i. 7
e. 1   j. 5

C. Vocabulary Practice

1. instantly
2. eager
3. terrifying, fury
4. hiss
5. passion

D. Word Forms

1. fury, furious
2. lazed, laziness
3. passionate, passion
4. satisfaction, satisfied
5. terrifying, terror

E. Language Activity: Imagery

1. c   3. c   5. a   7. b
2. a   4. c   6. a

7. PASTE

BEFORE YOU READ THE STORY

A. About the Author

(sample)

1. dissatisfaction with your own country; love for another country or culture; marriage/family ties; loss of citizenship in your own country.

Perhaps "love for another country" is most true of James. We know from the paragraph that he was partly educated in Europe and traveled there frequently. He may also simply not have liked living in the United States.

D. Scanning Different Sources of Information

1. Melville
2. Glaspell
3. Melville in New York City, Cather in Virginia, Glaspell in Davenport, Iowa, and James in Washington Place, New York

4. Cather
5. James
6. Europe: James; the sea: Melville; pioneers: Cather; Provincetown Playhouse: Glaspell

AFTER YOU READ THE STORY

A. Understanding the Plot

1. Arthur's stepmother has recently died. And just three weeks before that, his father had died.
2. He asks her to look at some of his stepmother's "things."
3. The "things" were jewels—"crowns and necklaces, diamonds and gold."
4. Arthur's stepmother had these things because before her marriage to Arthur's father she had been an actress, and the jewels were part of her costumes for the theater.
5. She finds a necklace of large pearls. She wonders if the pearls are possibly real.
6. Arthur gives the jewels to Charlotte. He is sure the jewels are not real because if his stepmother, who was poor, had been given real jewels when she was an actress, then, in Arthur's opinion, her virtue would not be "above question."
7. Mrs. Guy is organizing a play for the birthday of the son of the family Charlotte works for, and she needs something to "brighten up" the clothes the actors will wear. Charlotte shows her the jewels she was given by Arthur.
8. She tells Charlotte the pearls are real—and valuable.
9. Charlotte decides to return the pearls to Arthur and tell him that they are real.
10. He tells Charlotte, by letter, that the jeweler said the pearls were paste—that is, not real.
11. She says she bought them from the jeweler to whom Arthur sold them. She may have gotten them somehow from Arthur himself.

B. Close Reading

Part I
1. Charlotte
    a. She lives with a wealthy family as a governess for their children. She has no money of her own.

b. *Thoughtful.* In paragraphs 2 and 3, we see Charlotte
   thoughtfully considering Arthur's reaction to his
   stepmother's death. In paragraph 4, the jewels remind her
   of her uncle and his second wife, and she thinks about
   them. In paragraph 15, she continues to turn the jewels
   over in her hand, thinking about the woman who had
   once owned them.
   c. She is generally eager to please (see paragraphs 7, 21, 26,
   33–34, 42–44, 54, 56).

2. Arthur
   a. His father was a minister. His stepmother had been an
   actress. Arthur seems to have respect for her, if not love.
   She was his father's wife, and therefore her virtue is
   important to Arthur.
   b. He is not a man of strong feelings. Perhaps he is not even
   a man of genuine or honest feelings. He does not have a
   generous nature; it is difficult for him to perform an act
   of generosity.
   c. It is very important to Arthur that "Mama" was a
   woman of virtue. If the pearls are real, this could mean
   that she gave herself to a man in return for the jewelry.
   And this, in Arthur's opinion, would somehow make
   Arthur himself a lesser or less virtuous person.

Parts II and III

1. Mrs. Guy knows the pearls are real—and valuable. So she
   thinks Arthur must have been very kind indeed to give them
   to Charlotte; and maybe she even suspects that he has
   romantic feelings toward Charlotte.
2. She might have finished the sentence this way: ". . . then if I
   am an honest person, I must give them back."
3. Mrs. Guy feels Arthur had his chance to see that the pearls
   were real and that Charlotte behaved honestly in trying to
   make him see that they might be real. So now, in Mrs. Guy's
   opinion, Charlotte should keep them.
4. Mrs. Guy believes that Charlotte's stepaunt received the
   pearls from "an admirer"—a man who was in love with
   her.
5. She is probably both shocked and excited—shocked because
   she knows how much Arthur disapproves of such a
   possibility, and excited because the passions of love are
   attractive, although unknown to her.

6. Charlotte wants Arthur to believe that the pearls are *not* real because if he believes they are false, he will let her keep them; and now she is certain they are real. Arthur thinks that his stepmother, the actress, could have gotten real pearls only by acting in an "improper" way with an admirer; and this would make people think less of his father (a minister) for marrying such a woman.

C. Vocabulary Practice

1. b 3. a 5. b
2. c 4. b 6. c

D. Word Forms

1. apologetically
2. admission
3. Relief
4. possessive
5. disturbing

E. Language Activity: Overstatement

1. James suggests with this phrase that Mrs. Guy looks innocent but has much experience and a lot of strength. She may look "sweet," but she is also clever and not very sensitive to other people's feelings.
2. Mrs. Guy is organizing a play. She feels that the pearls are so beautiful that they have a story to tell and that they will give her (and her actors) ideas about how to play their parts in the play.
3. Mrs. Guy is saying here that pearls respond to human passions, human love, and that they don't "wake up"— don't show their beauty—until they are worn by someone who has a passionate character.

8. THE LOST PHOEBE

BEFORE YOU READ THE STORY

A. About the Author

His family was so poor that his parents had to separate from each other to support the children. Also, he lived in many different towns and states. These experiences might have helped him write about poor people and given him knowledge about people in general.

D. Skimming for the Basic Idea and Scanning for Information

(see answers to Understanding the Plot, below)

AFTER YOU READ THE STORY

A. Understanding the Plot

1. They had been married for forty-eight years.
2. Their marriage was a happy one. They were a loving couple.
3. They lived mainly alone, without much connection to their neighbors. Their children were dead or distant. In general, the rest of the world was far off.
4. After Phoebe dies, Henry imagines he sees her in and around the house.
5. He leaves home to find his lost Phoebe. His behavior is strange to us and to all the country people.
6. He searches for his lost Phoebe for several years (seven, to be exact.)
7. Phoebe appears before him in her youthful form, and, in trying to reach her, he jumps from the top of Red Cliff and dies.

B. Close Reading

Part I

1. The "new part" was added when Henry married Phoebe. Now it looked weather-beaten and old.
2. Cherry-wood cupboard, large bed, chest of drawers, carpet frame, doorless clothes-cupboard, broken mirror, hatstand, sewing machine. The carpet frame was used by Phoebe; the mirror broke three days before their youngest son died.
3. Moss covered the buildings and trees of the orchard.
4. "In fact, everything on the farm had aged and faded along with Old Henry and his wife Phoebe."
5. Three died, three lived at a distance, and the daughter who lived near them hardly gave them a thought.

6. They planted and harvested corn and wheat, took the grain to market, cut wood for fires, cooked, repaired things, visited.

Part II

1. d 3. b 5. d
2. d 4. b

Part III

(samples; there are several possible questions for each answer)

1. Where did Henry find shelter?
2. What did Henry call as he walked through the countryside?
3. Why would Henry occasionally throw his walking stick in front of him?
4. Where did Henry often spend the night in fair weather?
5. What effect had long walking and little eating had on Henry's body?
6. How did Phoebe appear to Henry at Red Cliff?
7. What had gone from Henry when he reached the edge of the cliff?
8. Where did Henry see Phoebe?
9. What did Henry feel as he called Phoebe's name?
10. Who knew how eagerly and happily Henry had found his lost Phoebe?

C. Vocabulary Practice: Understanding Words in Context

1. a 3. c 5. c
2. b 4. b

D. Word Forms

(sample sentences)

1. Henry's neighbors were astonished because he looked like a madman; yet they treated him with kindness.
2. Henry's condition saddened Mrs. Race, but she made him breakfast with an almost cheerful manner.
3. Phoebe's appearing to be alive was a hallucination, a product only of Henry's mind.
4. As a couple, Henry and Phoebe were not really quarrelsome; if Phoebe threatened to leave Henry, she did it only jokingly.

5. Having heard Henry's story about looking for Phoebe, Farmer Dodge could only stare wonderingly after the man when he walked down the road.
6. At the end of the story, Henry remembers Phoebe's pleasant way of smiling sympathetically.